EASTERN OREGON WILDERNESS AREAS

by
Donna Ikenberry Aitkenhead

Photographs by
Donna and Roger Aitkenhead

The Touchstone Press
P.O. Box 81
Beaverton, Oregon 97075

Cover photos: *Black Canyon Wilderness*
Wenaha River
Lookingglass Lake

I.S.B.N. 0-911518-81-9
Copyright © 1990
by Donna and Roger Aitkenhead
Maps courtesy U.S. Geological Survey

For
*Roger Aitkenhead, my husband, friend
and favorite backpacking companion.*

Donna and Sam at Nip and Tuck Pass

CONTENTS

- INTRODUCTION 7
- I. THE BLACK CANYON WILDERNESS 10
  1. Black Canyon Trail 13
- II. THE BRIDGE CREEK WILDERNESS 15
  2. Bridge Creek Trail 17
  3. North Point Trail 19
- III. THE EAGLE CAP WILDERNESS 20
  4. West Eagle Creek Trailhead to Traverse Lake 25
  5. Main Eagle Creek Trailhead to Eagle Lake 26
  6. Main Eagle Creek Trailhead to Lookingglass Lake 28
  7. Pine Lakes Trail 30
  8. Hidden Lake 31
  9. Jim White Ridge Loop 33
  10. Swamp Lake/Steamboat Lake/John Henry Lake Loop 35
- IV. THE HELLS CANYON WILDERNESS 39
  11. McGraw Cabin Loop 44
  12. Nee-Me-Poo Trail 46
  13. Dug Bar Trailhead to Deep Creek Ranch 48
  14. Freezeout Trailhead to Bear Mountain 50
  15. Freezeout Trailhead to Hat Point 52
  16. Western Rim/Hat Point/High Trail Loop 54
  17. Freezeout Trailhead to the Snake River (via Saddle Creek) ... 56
  18. Saddle Creek/Sluice Creek/Hat Point Loop 58
- V. THE MILL CREEK WILDERNESS 60
  19. Twin Pillars National Recreation Trail 62
  20. Wildcat Trail 64
  21. Belknap Trail 65
- VI. THE MONUMENT ROCK WILDERNESS 66
  22. Monument Rock Trail 69
  23. Little Malheur River Trail 70
- VII. THE NORTH FORK JOHN DAY WILDERNESS 71
  24. Glade Creek/Cold Spring Loop 76
  25. Olive Lake/Saddle Ridge/Lost Creek Loop 77
  26. North Fork John Day River Campground to Wind Rock 79
  27. Granite Creek Trailhead to the North Fork John Day River ... 81
  28. Elkhorn Crest Trail 83
  29. Crawfish Lake Trail 85
- VIII. THE NORTH FORK UMATILLA WILDERNESS 86
  30. Buck Creek Trail 89
  31. Ninemile Ridge Trail 91
  32. North Fork Umatilla River Trail 92
- IX. THE STRAWBERRY MOUNTAIN WILDERNESS 94
  33. Strawberry Campground to Strawberry Mountain 98
  34. Strawberry Campground to High Lake 100
  35. Little Riner/Mud Lake Loop 102
  36. Canyon Creek to Indian Creek Butte 104
- X. THE WENAHA-TUCANNON WILDERNESS 106
  37. Cross Creek Trailhead to Wenaha River 108
  38. Elk Flat Trailhead to the Wenaha River 109
  39. Timothy Spring Trailhead to Wenaha River/Milk Creek 110
- ACKNOWLEDGEMENTS 112

Roger and Sam at Strawberry Lake

INTRODUCTION

Oregon is known for its spectacular coastline, splendid Cascade Mountains, and for the fertile valleys that lie between the Coast Range and the Cascades. In the eastern portion of the state sagebrush and bitterbrush blanket the land, the Wallowa Mountains reach for the sky, and the Blue Mountains stretch out across wide open places. In addition to all of this, visitors will find several wilderness areas just waiting to be explored.

There are currently 37 wilderness areas in Oregon, 10 of which are located in the eastern half of the state. Reaching from the Ochoco National Forest near Prineville, to the Oregon/Idaho border, then north to the Oregon/Washington border, eastern Oregon's wildernesses offer a multitude of scenes to view, things to do, and plenty of room to roam.

Statewide there are over two million acres of designated wilderness. The ten areas in this guidebook total 907,495 acres, or nearly one-half of the state total.

Eastern Oregon has much to offer. There are tall granite peaks, high mountain lakes, and rushing streams in Eagle Cap Wilderness, located in the Wallowa Mountains. Some say the area resembles the Swiss Alps. Many agree. And to the east of Eagle Cap, one can hike down into Hells Canyon, the deepest gorge in North America.

When the word "wilderness" is mentioned to some folks, they envision themselves at a city park located in the middle of one of America's largest cities. Others imagine a hike through the nearby woods, a trip to Yellowstone National Park, or maybe a weekend at a local campground. But "wilderness", as defined in this book, includes areas designated by Congress as a result of the Wilderness Act of 1964.

Throughout the United States there are over thirty-two million acres of wilderness under the National Wilderness Preservation System. According to the law, wilderness "shall be administered for the use and enjoyment of the American People in such a manner as will leave them unimpaired for future use and enjoyment as wilderness, and so as to provide for the protection of these areas (and) the preservation of their wilderness character."

But "wilderness character" is becoming much more difficult to protect. Why? Because, we are loving the wilderness to death. Many areas suffer because of overcrowding. People flock together, instead of spreading out. And many times, we travel familiar trails instead of exploring someplace new.

In this guidebook, we've included some trails that receive a bit more use than we'd like, but most of the time we've explored trails that receive little use. Whenever possible, we've avoided those areas that are overcrowded, overused, those that take away from a "true wilderness experience."

Managed for its pristine character, wilderness is a place where one can experience risk, beauty, and solitude. It's a place "where man is a visitor who does not remain," and a place where certain rules must be adhered to. The "No Trace" concept can and must be taught to people of all ages, for if we fail to do so, the wilderness will die. Everyone should learn to "Take only pictures; leave only footprints."

This means that flowers are to be seen and not picked. If you want a souvenir, take a photograph. It'll last much longer than a flower that will soon die. And Indian artifacts are to be looked at, then left alone.

In regards to leaving footprints, hikers are advised to plow right through muddy trails. Detouring around a soggy portion will only increase the damage and worsen the impact. If traveling cross-country, especially if in a group, spread out rather than walking one behind the other. A line of hikers traveling through tundra or meadows can crush plant tissue beyond recovery and create channels for erosion.

Use a campsite that has already been trampled down instead of crushing untouched vegetation. Avoid fragile shores of lakes and streams. Instead, pitch a tent or throw out your sleeping bag on a ridgetop. Often these spots have fewer bugs because they catch more of a breeze.

Always choose a campsite more than 100 feet from water and avoid camping in meadows. Please note: Some wilderness areas require choosing a site a minimum distance of 200 feet from a water source. Check with the Forest Service managing the area you plan to visit for more details.

All backpackers should carry a portable camp stove. Leaving no trace whatsoever, camp stoves are small, efficient, lightweight, and easy to use. Those who insist on building a campfire should do so only when dead wood is available on the ground, and all fires should be completely out before leaving the campsite. In some areas there are restrictions regarding campfires. Please check with the managing Forest for up-to-date information.

All garbage should be packed out and never buried. Wild animals will soon dig it up. (Also, do not feed the wildlife.) Unfortunately, there are those who insist on littering the trails with beverage cans and candy bar wrappers. Remember, pack out what you pack in. Because the contents have already been consumed, trash is much lighter, making it real simple for those that care. Also, those burning their trash should remember that cans and foil do not burn.

Bathing and washing clothes should be done away from streams, springs, and lakes. Soap, including the biodegradable variety, should never be used near a water source (stay at least 100 feet away). And always bury your toothpaste.

To dispose of human waste, use the "cat method." Dig a hole six to eight inches deep, placing the top soil to one side. (A light garden trowel works well.) After use, fill the hole with loose soil then tramp in the top soil. And cover with a rock if possible.

Primitive methods of travel are allowed in the wilderness. These include backpacking, day hiking, or riding a horse. Other methods of travel include using a pack animal such as a horse, mule, llama, or you can do like us and bring along a backpacking canine. Mechanical or motorized methods of travel are not allowed. These include motorcycles and mountain bikes.

I know there are those who object to dogs being allowed in the wilderness, but there are those who'd rather have dogs in the wilderness than people. How many times I've heard, "Well, at least dogs do not litter or throw beer cans on the trail." And others claim that dogs bark, chase wildlife, etc. Of course this is true, but only if the dog is not restrained. Keep your pet quiet, use a leash to keep him or her under control, and there should be no problem at all. Those that do not want to leash their pets or keep them quiet should leave their animals at home.

Hikers will occasionally meet people on horseback in the wilderness and should know that they are expected to give the horseback rider the right of way. In fact, hikers should remember to remain on the down side of the trail when meeting riders on the trail.

Horseback riders should note that a limit of 10 or 12 persons/animal groups are allowed in the wilderness. For example, one can have a group of six people and six pack animals, or eight people and four pack animals. Stock owners should note that feed should be carried and animals should be picketed at least 200 feet from any water source.

Some folks enter the wilderness with the thought of hunting or fishing. Those interested in such activities will have to purchase permits and obtain up-to-date information on opening and closing dates.

While hiking throughout the wilderness it's easy to think of the many springs, streams and rivers as being clear and pure. But often they are not. Some of the waters are plagued with the parasite Giardia lamblia, also known as "backpackers' diarrhea."

Hikers will want to be cautious of all water sources, even those that feel cold, look pure, smell clean, and taste fine. And if two people drink from the same Giardia-infested water source, one may end up with Giardia, while the other may show no symptoms whatsoever. Those infected with Giardia may suffer from diarrhea, loss of appetite, abdominal cramps, gas and bloating.

There are several ways to avoid the disease. First of all, boil all water. Some sources recommend boiling water a minimum of one minute at altitudes below 4,000 feet. At higher altitudes boil water for a longer period of time. And others recommend boiling all water for 10 minutes, regardless of the altitude. There are several other methods of treating water. These include water purifiers and commercial water purification chemicals, but note that these are not always effective in killing the organisms.

Now that the rules for wilderness travel are clear, you'll want to grab your pack and head for the hills. And by following the above suggestions you'll insure a "true wilderness experience" for generations to come. May God be with you during your many travels.

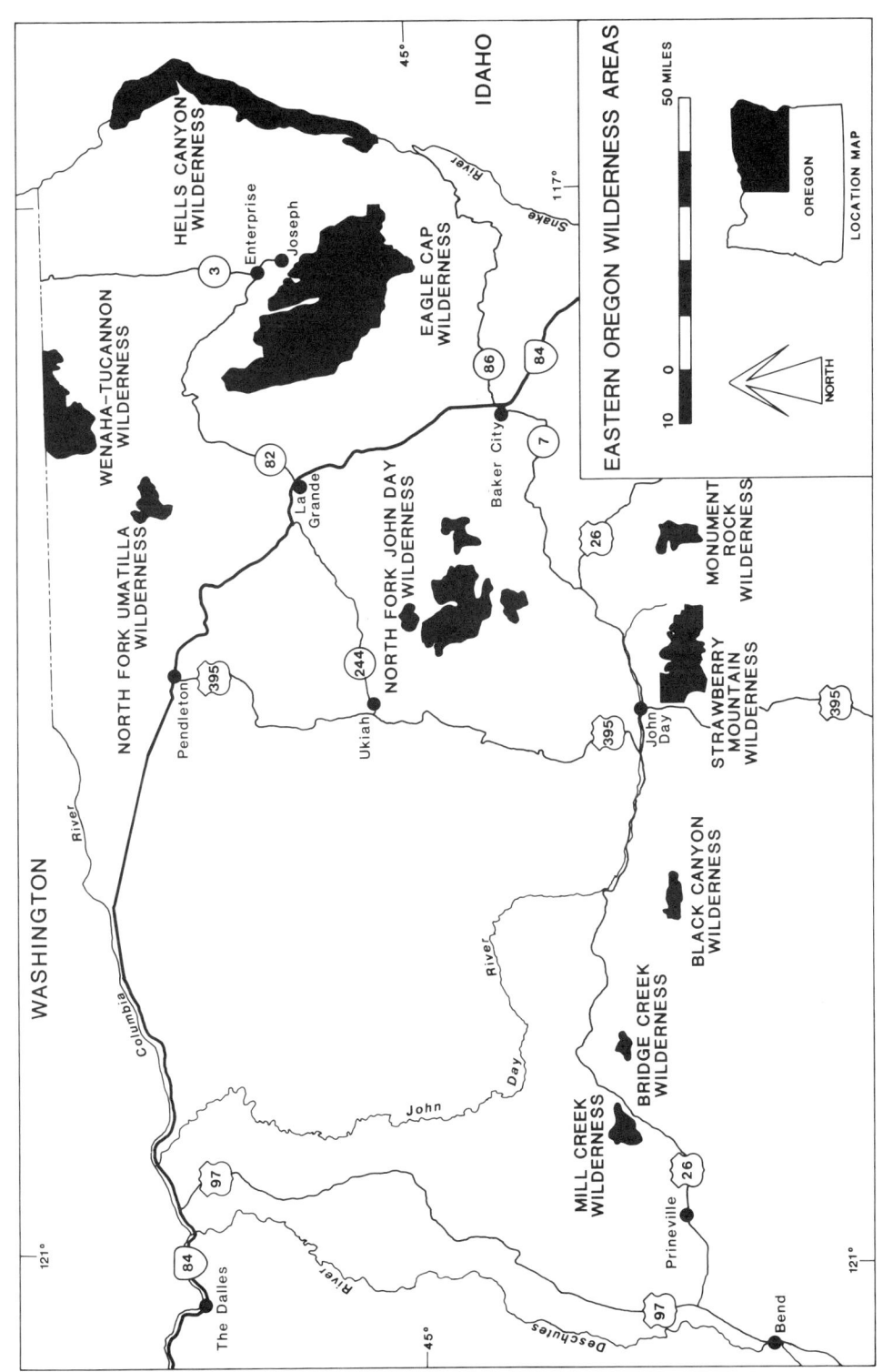

INTRODUCTION TO THE BLACK CANYON WILDERNESS

Steep canyons, sharp ridges, tree-covered mesas, wildflowers, and an abundance of wildlife can all be found in Black Canyon Wilderness. Solitude can be enjoyed if one visits during the spring and summer season, before hunters invade the area in the fall.

Black Canyon Wilderness is located near the center of Oregon, 57 miles east of Prineville, and 35 miles west of John Day. Comprised of approximately 13,400 acres, the area was designated as such by Congress with the passage of the Oregon Wilderness Act of 1984.

Managed exclusively by the Ochoco National Forest, the area was first considered for wilderness classification for several reasons. "It met criteria for remoteness, solitude and size," writes Arthur J. Currier, Acting District Ranger for the Paulina Ranger District, Ochoco National Forest. In addition, Currier claims, "It is a watershed which has had little direct human-caused impacts. It was also representative of a variety of Central Oregon vegetation types."

Black Canyon Creek drains through the Wilderness from the west to the east, dropping over 3,000 feet in the process. As it nears its low point in the east, Black Canyon Creek flows into the South Fork of the John Day River. Anglers should note that the best fishing occurs early in the season for Black Canyon Creek is a fairly small stream. The fish tend to be small as well.

Seventeen miles of trails traverse the Wilderness, most of which are maintained whenever funding permits. Elevation in the area varies with the lowest point of 2,850 feet located at the eastern boundary where Black Canyon Creek joins the South Fork of the John Day River on Bureau of Land Management land. The highest point, 6,483 feet, is located near Wolf Mountain Lookout. Located a few hundred feet outside the Wilderness, the Lookout provides a great view and is currently manned each summer.

A wide range in elevation provides a variety of terrain to explore. Volcanic ash soils cover about one-third of the area with nearly one-half of the Wilderness devoid of trees. Most of these non-timbered openings are located on ridge tops or south facing slopes. Northern slopes generally support a forest of mixed conifers, and southern slopes usually contain a mixture of ponderosa pine, juniper, and mixed conifers. Over fifty percent of the timbered sections are considered old-growth forest.

Snow and cold temperatures invade each winter, but the area is usually snowfree around June of each year and normally remains open until the beginning of November. Temperatures vary in this part of Oregon, with daytime summer highs ranging from the low 40's to the high 90's. But, 70's and 80's are typical. Nighttime lows, during the summer months, usually dip to anywhere between 30 and 60 degrees. Winter temperatures range from the teen's to the 40's during the day with nights 20 to 40 degrees colder.

Wildlife and wildflowers abound although flowers are much more easily observed. Wild animals tend to be very shy, but still it is exciting just knowing they are there. Three hundred species of wildlife are common to the Ochoco National Forest, most of which may exist in the Wilderness. Common big game species include elk and deer. Also, there may be the chance to see the rarely-observed mountain lion which is believed to inhabit the area as well. Other species include, black bear, coyotes, marmots, porcupines, and badgers. Of course, the bird life found here is equally exciting.

Rattlesnakes are one species of animal life that hikers should be aware of. Mosquitoes do not appear to be a problem.

A variety of wildflowers paint the area during the early summer months. The Forest Service recommends viewing wildflowers before July, as Central Oregon's hot dry days and fairly cool nights force flowers to bloom just after snowmelt.

Those looking for flowers, solitude, and a true wilderness experience, will want to visit Black Canyon prior to the fall hunting season.

For more information contact the following:

Ochoco National Forest	or	Ochoco National Forest
Paulina Ranger District		P.O. Box 490
HC 68, Box 6015		Prineville, OR 97754
Paulina, OR 97751		(503) 447-6247

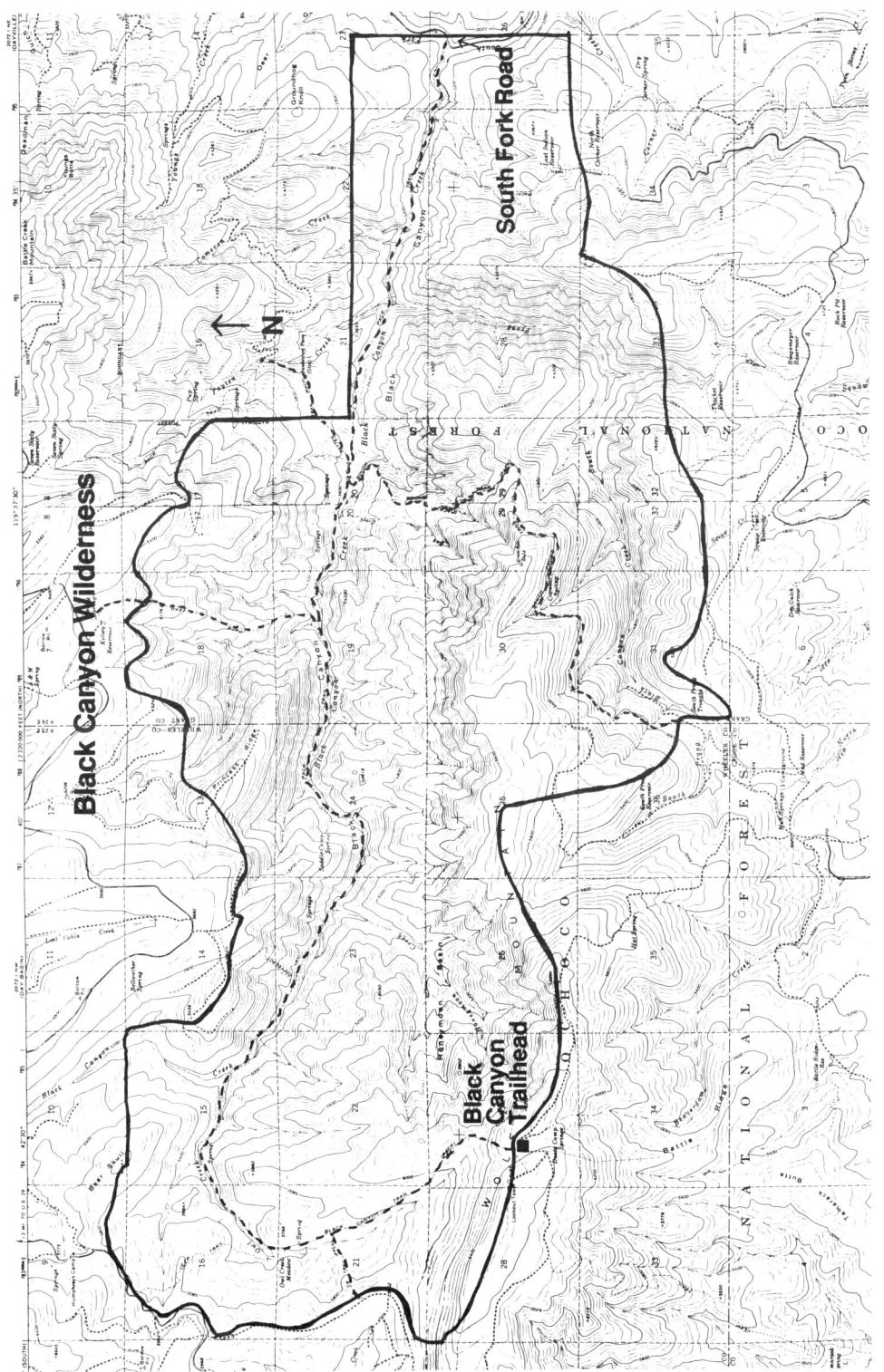

EASTERN OREGON WILDERNESS AREAS

Black Canyon Creek

1 BLACK CANYON TRAIL

Distance: 11.6 miles (one-way)
Elevation gain: 200 feet; loss 3,750 feet
High point: 6,400 feet
Usually open: June through November
Topographic map: U.S.G.S. Wolf Mountain, OR - 1972
Obtain map from: U.S.G.S. — Denver, Colorado

Hiking the Black Canyon Trail provides the opportunity to hike through old-growth forest of Douglas fir and ponderosa pine, and allows one to enjoy Black Canyon Creek.

Black Canyon flows from near the west end of the Wilderness to the east end where it joins the South Fork of the John Day River. Besides scenic value, the area also offers the chance to observe animal life and a variety of wildflowers during the late spring/early summer. Best of all, you can experience solitude. Those who love to get their feet wet will think this is heaven as you must ford Owl Creek once and Black Canyon Creek 20 times. Also, it's necessary to hop across numerous other small streams and springs.

There are several ways to reach the Black Canyon Trailhead, two of which follow. Both routes are scenic, the first traveling through miles of forest, the second passing through some forest, then out onto the main highway, U.S. Hwy. 26.

To reach the trailhead drive 17.0 miles east from the junction of U.S. Hwy. 26 and U.S. Hwy. 126 in Prineville, Oregon (supplies available). Turn right off U.S. Hwy. 26 onto a paved road where a sign reads, "Ochoco R.S." Continue to a fork 8.7 miles down the road and head right on paved FS Road No. 42. Drive 23.5 miles farther to Deep Creek Campground, a place where free campsites abound, complete with picnic tables and pit toilets.

From the campground continue another 12.9 miles and turn left at the junction, then make a quick right onto FS Road No. 12. (Three miles prior to the junction the road turns from paved into a good gravel road.)

From this point drive 1.4 miles and reach a fork in the road. Stay straight on FS Road No. 38. Turn right on FS Road No. 3810 located another 2.1 miles down the road then turn left on FS Road No. 500, a dirt road, 1.1 miles farther. Continue 3.9 miles turning left on FS Road No. 5810 (no sign) then reach a fork another 0.6 mile up the road, now traveling on FS Road No. 5820. At 0.4 mile turn right on FS Road No. 5840. Reach the Wolf Mountain lookout 2.3 miles away. The trailhead is located another 0.2 mile down the road. There is room to park and also to camp if an early start is desired.

To reach the trailhead via the second route drive 63 miles east on U.S. Hwy. 26 from Prineville, Oregon, and turn right on FS Road No. 12. Follow the road (paved for 5.8 miles, good gravel for the remainder) to the junction of FS Road No. 1250 at 15.6 miles.

Turn left, driving Road No. 1250 for 3.9 miles. Then head straight at the junction, now driving FS Road No. 090. Now the road is rocky, but passable in good weather via passenger car. Stay on Road No. 090 for 3.6 miles then turn left on FS Road No. 5820. Continue another 0.4 mile to FS Road No. 5840. Drive this 2.5 miles to the trailhead.

Begin hiking Black Canyon Trail No. 820 descending through the trees or semi-open slope at a gradual (occasionally steep) grade to a junction at 1.5 miles. Continue straight, shortly thereafter hiking on the slope above Owl Creek.

Now descend at a gradual rate, hiking through lush vegetation to an unsigned junction at 1.9 miles. Stay straight, reaching a short spur trail to Owl Creek and a good spot for water at 2.7 miles.

Cross Owl Creek at 3.0 miles and descend moderately to Black Canyon Creek at 3.2 miles. Ford the creek and cross again at 3.4 miles now hiking level or gradually up and down.

Throughout the trip there are numerous wildflowers to enjoy including such colorful species as columbine, ladys-slipper, lupine, and paintbrush. Also, there are a variety of ferns and many kinds of trees.

In addition, there are numerous kinds of animal species to observe. There are elk, deer, porcupine, and many birds. Watch for rattlesnakes. We saw two while hiking a one-quarter mile stretch of trail.

Cross two streams, one at 4.5 miles and another at 4.6 miles, then head down and across Black Canyon Creek at 5.0 miles, now hiking the north side of the creek. Cross to the south side of the creek at 5.2 miles then back to the north, reaching a camp and signs "Wheeler County Line" and "Grant County Line" at 6.2 miles.

After this point the trail climbs moderately up the semi-open slope, taking the hiker above the creek, then descending at a moderate to steep grade and back down near the creek. From up on the slope notice the nice view to the east and of the drainage itself.

Cross the stream at 7.0 miles then gradually descend and reach a camp in the trees at 7.5 miles. This is a fairly good camp with creek water available. Also there are three springs located just down the trail from the camp.

Gradually descend or remain level across the semi-open area and reach a camp among a few ponderosas at 8.1 miles. This camp is also near Black Canyon Creek. Continue to 8.2 miles and the junction to Payten Trail No. 820D.

At 8.8 and 8.9 miles cross streams, hiking through the trees some of the time, across semi-open slope the remainder of the time. At 9.4 miles cross Payten Creek.

Now begin a series of creek crossings, 14 in the next two miles to be exact. Ford Black Canyon Creek at 9.7 miles and again at 9.8 miles. Then hop across Cameron Creek at 9.9 miles. Again ford Black Canyon Creek at 10.0 miles, 10.2 miles, and once again 100 feet or so down river. Cross eight more times, ending on the north side of the creek at 11.1 miles.

At 11.3 miles head south across the creek then north again and reach the South Fork John Day River at 11.6 miles. Those with a shuttle available can ford the South Fork John Day River and have a car waiting on South Fork Road, located on Bureau of Land Management land.

Lupines in Black Canyon Wilderness

INTRODUCTION TO THE BRIDGE CREEK WILDERNESS

Of Oregon's 37 designated wilderness areas, Bridge Creek Wilderness has the distinction of being the third smallest. Steep terrain, open meadows, forested slopes, and scab flats, also known as plateaus, in addition to solitude and great views, combine to make this area a nice place to visit.

Bridge Creek was designated a wilderness in 1984 when the Oregon Wilderness Act was signed by President Reagan. Chosen for it's excellent wildlife habitat according to the Forest Service, 5,380 acre Bridge Creek is located 30 miles east/northeast of Prineville, Oregon.

A 3.5 mile trail penetrates the preserve but the trail is not maintained and there are no plans to upgrade it. Also, there is an old road which leads one mile to North Point and a spectacular view. The Forest Service has chosen to manage the area as a trailless wilderness. The area ranges in elevation from 4,360 feet at the northern boundary to 6,607 feet at the southern boundary near Carroll Camp.

A mixed conifer forest of white fir, Douglas-fir, western larch, and some lodgepole pine and ponderosa pine cover about four-fifths of the area with one-fifth of the wilderness being open. In addition, there are sagebrush, snowberry, and other brush species.

There are 5.8 miles of streams with Bridge Creek (good fishing reported here) flowing through the center of the Wilderness in a south to north direction. At one time Bridge Creek was a water source for the small community of Mitchell, located to the north. Today, however, the community depends on wells and springs instead of Bridge Creek. Other water sources in the area include Maxwell Creek and five springs: Thompson, Pisgah, Masterson, Nelson, and Maxwell.

Hikers will find July, August, September, and October, the best times for visiting. Snow makes access difficult during late fall, winter, and early spring.

Bridge Creek is rarely crowded, but in the fall it becomes a popular hunting area. An excellent elk wintering area, the Wilderness is used by some elk throughout the year. Other large mammals found in the area include mule deer, bear and mountain lion.

Several unique species of bird life may also be seen as pileated woodpeckers, goshawks, and prairie falcons nest within the Wilderness. To date, there have been no sightings of any endangered species.

For more information contact the following:

Big Summit Ranger District
Ochoco National Forest
HC 69, Box 255
Prineville, OR 97754

or

Forest Supervisor
Ochoco National Forest
P.O. Box 490
Prineville, OR 97754

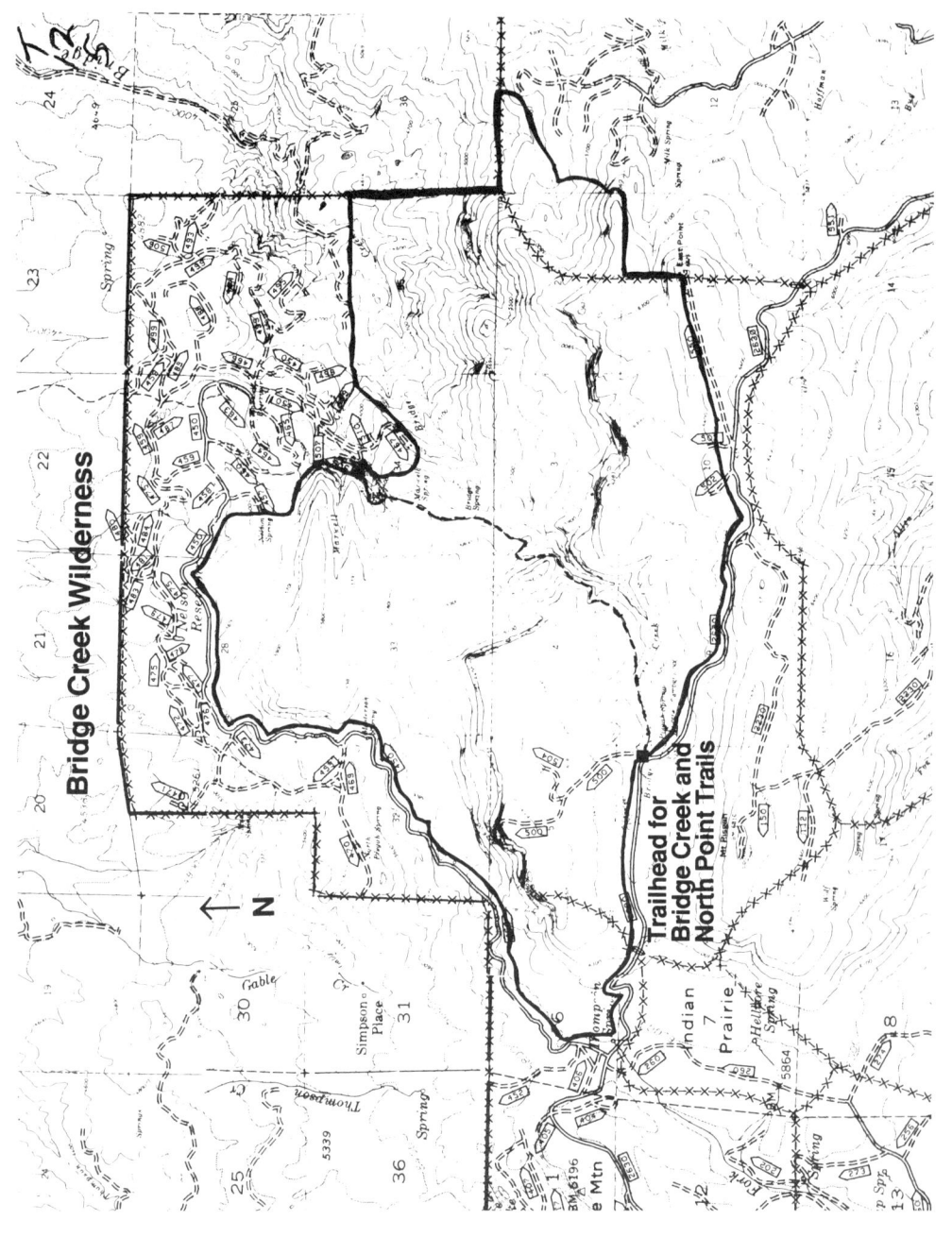

2 BRIDGE CREEK TRAIL

Distance: 3.5 miles (one-way)
Elevation gain: 1,200 feet; loss 100 feet
High Point: 6,200 feet
Usually open: July through October
Topographic map: U.S.G.S. Mt. Pisgah, OR. — 1966
Obtain map from: U.S.G.S. — Denver, Colorado

Although this trail is found on some maps, the newer maps have omitted it as it is no longer maintained. We hiked a portion of the trail but then it became more and more difficult to follow as fallen trees lay in our path.

The trail starts near Carroll Camp, a primitive camp with water available at Pisgah Spring. The first portion of the trail leads across meadows, along Bridge Creek, then up across an open ridge where there is a good view. Later the trail heads down into the trees, crossing two springs before ending at the northern boundary of the Wilderness.

To reach the trailhead drive 17 miles east on U.S. Hwy. 26 from the junction of U.S. Hwy. 26 and U.S. Hwy. 126 in Prineville, Oregon. Prineville is a small town with gas, food, and other supplies. Turn right on the paved road (sign states: "Ochoco R.S.") and follow this for 8.7 miles. At this point turn left on FS Road No. 22, driving past Walton Lake and continuing to the end of pavement at 8.1 miles.

Head to the left, now driving FS Road No. 150. Curve to the right at 0.8 mile now traveling on FS Road No. 2630. Reach Thompson Spring 3.7 miles farther and a sign for Bridge Creek Wilderness. Continue straight and reach Bridge Creek and an old road (trailhead) at 2.0 miles. Carroll Camp and Pisgah Spring is located 0.2 mile down the road.

Begin hiking the trail by traveling through the trees and the meadow to the east. Follow the blazed trees when necessary. At 0.1 mile the trail is a bit easier to follow.

Continue along, sometimes in the open or semi-open, staying on the north side of Bridge Creek. At 0.5 mile cross a small stream and head up the ridge to the old rock cairn.

Now you're hiking at a gradual rate through sagebrush and bitterbrush, and in the early summer you'll undoubtedly see plenty of wildflowers as well. The trail levels off soon after then descends via a switchback, heading into the trees at 0.8 mile.

Hike back out across an open slope with good views of the surrounding Wilderness and places beyond. At 1.5 miles the trail became more and more littered with fallen trees and we turned back. The map shows the trail continuing for another 2.0 miles. Those with the inclinations to bushwhack should have a great time!

View from North Point

3 NORTH POINT TRAIL

Distance: 1.0 mile (one-way)
Elevation gain: 340 feet; loss 0 feet
High point: 6,540 feet
Usually open: July through October
Topographic map: U.S.G.S. Mt. Pisgah, OR — 1966
Obtain map from: U.S.G.S. — Denver, Colorado

This trail isn't really a trail, instead it is an old road that at one time led to a lookout at North Point. The view is fantastic from this site, but the lookout was replaced with the one visible to the south on Mt. Pisgah.

The trail starts near Carroll Camp, a primitive camp with water available at Pisgah Spring. The first portion of the trail leads across meadows, along Bridge Creek, then up across an open ridge where there is a good view. Later the trail heads down into the trees, crossing two springs before ending at the northern boundary of the Wilderness.

To reach the trailhead drive 17 miles east on U.S. Hwy. 26 from the junction of U.S. Hwy. 26 and U.S. Hwy. 126 in Prineville, Oregon. Prineville is a small town with gas, food, and other supplies. Turn right on the paved road (sign states: "Ochoco R.S.") and follow this for 8.7 miles. At this point turn left on FS Road No. 22, driving past Walton Lake and continuing to the end of pavement at 8.1 miles.

Head to the left, now driving FS Road No. 150. Curve to the right at 0.8 mile now traveling on FS Road No. 2630. Reach Thompson Spring 3.7 miles farther and a sign for Bridge Creek Wilderness. Continue straight and reach Bridge Creek and an old road (trailhead) at 2.0 miles. Carroll Camp and Pisgah Spring is located 0.2 mile down the road.

Begin hiking the road, heading north for the 1.0 mile trek to North Point. The road is lined with thick pines, good habitat for grouse which we observed while hiking this trail.

From North Point the view is terrific with the Cascade Range visible to the west. Portions of Bridge Creek Wilderness and other points can be viewed as well.

Aspens near Bridge Creek

EASTERN OREGON WILDERNESS AREAS

INTRODUCTION TO THE EAGLE CAP WILDERNESS

Eagle Cap Wilderness! A land of high granite peaks, alpine lakes and meadows, steep glaciated valleys, abundant wildlife, delicate wildflowers, and spectacular vistas.

Comprised of most of the Wallowa Mountain Range, a spur of the Blue Mountains of northeastern Oregon, Eagle Cap Wilderness is bordered by Hells Canyon National Recreation Area on the southeast corner. In addition, the area is surrounded by other Wallowa-Whitman National Forest lands on all remaining sides.

Managed exclusively by the Wallowa-Whitman National Forest, the Wilderness was originally established as such by the Secretary of Agriculture on October 7, 1940. At that time, 220,000 acres were set aside. Later, Eagle Cap became part of the National Wilderness Preservation System under the Wilderness Act of 1964.

Today Oregon's largest wilderness consists of 358,461 acres with over 500 miles of trail providing access to this stunning area. Hikers can climb to the top of some of the highest peaks in the Wallowa Mountains, relax by 58 popular lakes or one of the many unnamed small lakes or tarns—many set in glacial cirques—and those who enjoy bushwhacking can climb to 8,800 feet and Legore Lake, Oregon's second highest lake.

Anglers will find good fishing in many area lakes with eastern brook, rainbow, or golden trout available. Also, there are four major rivers to fish, as well as numerous creeks and streams. Flowing from the slopes of Eagle Cap are the Minam, Lostine, Wallowa, and Imnaha rivers, where one can hook rainbow and eastern brook trout. In addition, most large streams contain anadromous fish habitat with species such as steelhead and spring and fall chinook. And all provide fishing that's been rated good to excellent.

Rock climbers will find several opportunities for climbing with Eagle Cap Peak, Matterhorn, and Sacajawea being the most popular. Those in search of a less crowded peak to climb should note that there are 31 peaks over 8,000 feet in elevation. Two peaks, Matterhorn and Sacajawea soar to nearly 10,000 feet, 15 more climb to over 9,000 feet, and 14 others reach more than 8,000 feet.

While hiking the trails throughout the area it's interesting to note that many of them originated from wildlife and American Indian paths. Used as hunting and plant gathering grounds, native Americans did not live in the area year-round because of the harsh conditions. In the late 1800's, the trails were improved by sheepmen, trappers, and prospectors. Today, mining relics can be found in some areas.

While hiking has proven to be the most popular wilderness pastime, there are other activities to enjoy as well. Besides fishing and rock climbing, there is horseback riding, photography, and during the winter months, cross-country skiing and snowshoeing. In addition, there are two activities which make a true wilderness experience perhaps the most pleasurable of all—wildlife viewing and plant study.

Supporting nearly every plant community present in the Blue Mountains, Eagle Cap Wilderness and the Lower Minam are truly a plant-lover's delight. At low elevations is bunchgrass and sagebrush. Higher up grows spruce, subalpine fir, and grouse huckleberry. Also, ponderosa pine, mountain hemlock, and several small stands of limber pine. Above treeline plant communities are dominated by subalpine shrubs, heather, sedges, and fragile alpine plants bred to withstand severe conditions.

Ranging from a low of 4,000 to 5,000 feet along the lower river drainages to a high of 9,839 feet atop Sacajawea Mountain, the Wilderness embraces a variety of habitat types which provide good opportunities for native wildlife species. Elk or deer may be seen in most parts of the area during summer and fall with elk wintering on the lower Eagle Cap winter ranges. Other species that might be observed include: black bear, cougar, bobcat, bighorn sheep, coyotes, bats, hoary marmots, flying squirrels, porcupine, otter, beaver, badgers, and wolverine. Also, there are mountain goats. Introduced on Chief Joseph Mountain in March of 1950, the herd has increased and appears to have stabilized. The goats are most often seen at Chief Joseph Mountain, as well as Ice Lake, the Matterhorn, and Sacajawea Peak.

Bird life in the area is equally as impressive with blue grouse, Clark's nutcrackers, and a variety of species of woodpeckers, owls, and sandpipers sighted. Peregrine falcons have also been observed, an endangered species capable of diving up to 200 mph in pursuit of prey.

During the winter bald eagles may be seen, another species that is threatened in Oregon. Also, golden eagles, Swainson's hawks, ferruginous hawks, and many other species of raptors.

Although the human population doesn't surpass the animal and bird population it may seem so at times. But, don't be discouraged. Popular, spectacular, and attractive, Eagle Cap Wilderness offers both crowds and solitude. First of all, unless you're looking for swarms of people skip the Lakes Basin. The most heavily used area, Lakes Basin visitors will find campfire closures in effect year-round, and a double set of wilderness guards on duty everyday, 24 hours per day, throughout the summer. A number of alpine lakes dot the area with an average of three to four camps surrounding each lake and about four people per camp. And this is on a weekday. Of course weekends are even busier, with the Forest Service counting up to 70 people at Minam Lake alone. Because we don't believe in attracting more people to an already overcrowded area we avoided the Lakes Basin.

Those choosing solitude over crowds will find a wide variety of places to visit. While backpacking through the areas listed in this book we occasionally met other hikers. But we found lonely lakes to camp at each night, and only once had to share a lake with two other couples. The rest of the time we were alone. Bushwhacking opportunities are plentiful as well. Check your wilderness map or with the Forest Service for more information.

Eagle Cap Wilderness is usually accessible by the Fourth of July, but mountain passes often support snowdrifts until August. The hiking season is short, as heavy snows usually hit the area by late October. Temperatures vary in the summer with highs warming to the 90's at times and dropping to the 40's at night. Visitors should be prepared for sudden changes in the weather and look out for late-afternoon thunderstorms.

Mosquitoes and horseflies are reported to be a problem when the temperature climbs although our backpacking trips during the months of July and August were bug-free. Bring insect repellant just in case.

Those who enjoy being pampered may want to contact one of several local outfitters and guides who rent out pack and saddle stock on a daily basis. In addition, they will pack parties to the campsite of your choice, cater to groups on trips of several days or more, and operate some spike, base, and drop camps.

For more information contact the following:

Wallowa-Whitman National Forest
P.O. Box 907
Baker, Oregon 97814
(503) 523-6391

or

Eagle Cap Ranger District
P.O. Box M
Enterprise, Oregon 97828

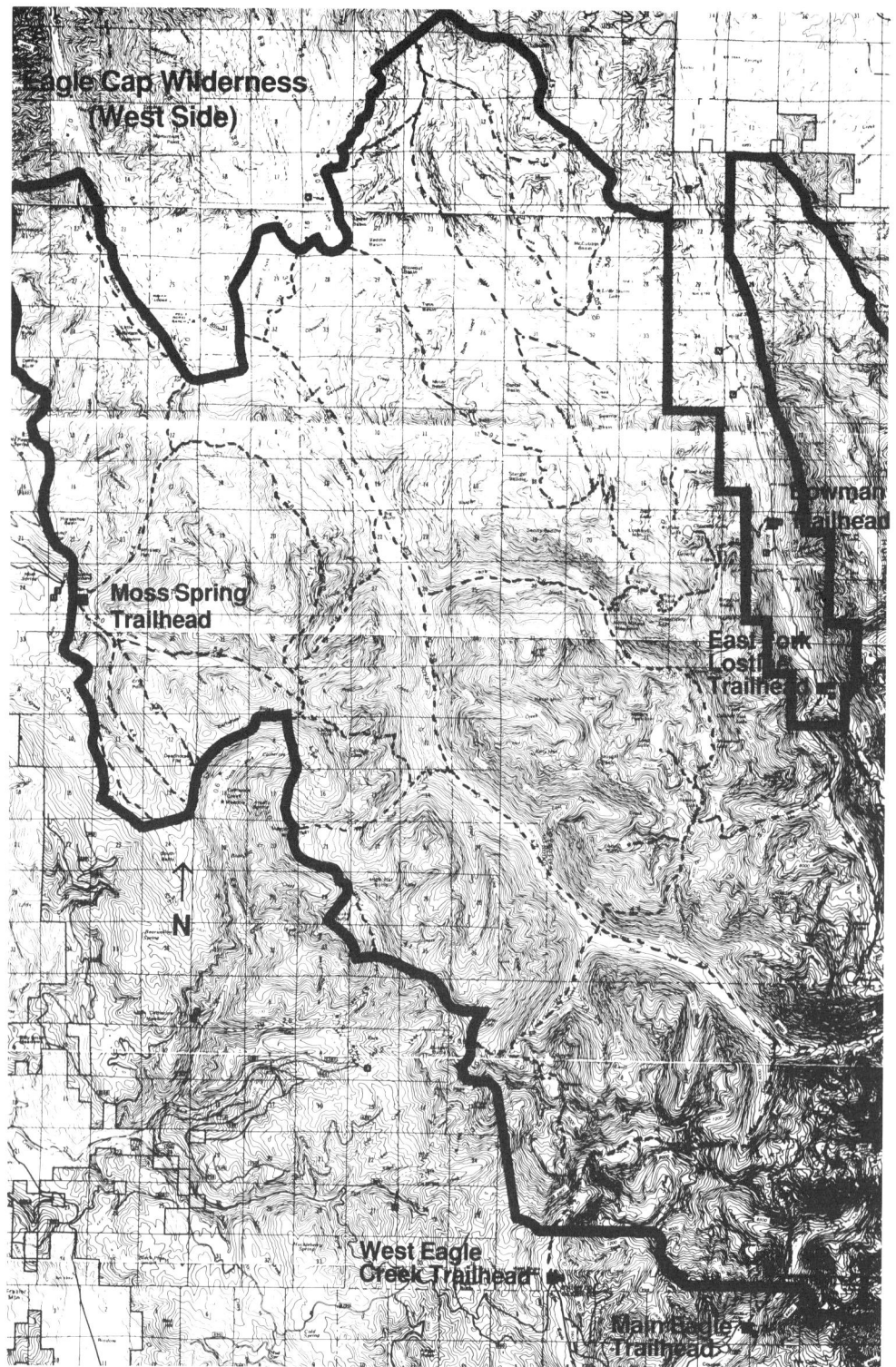

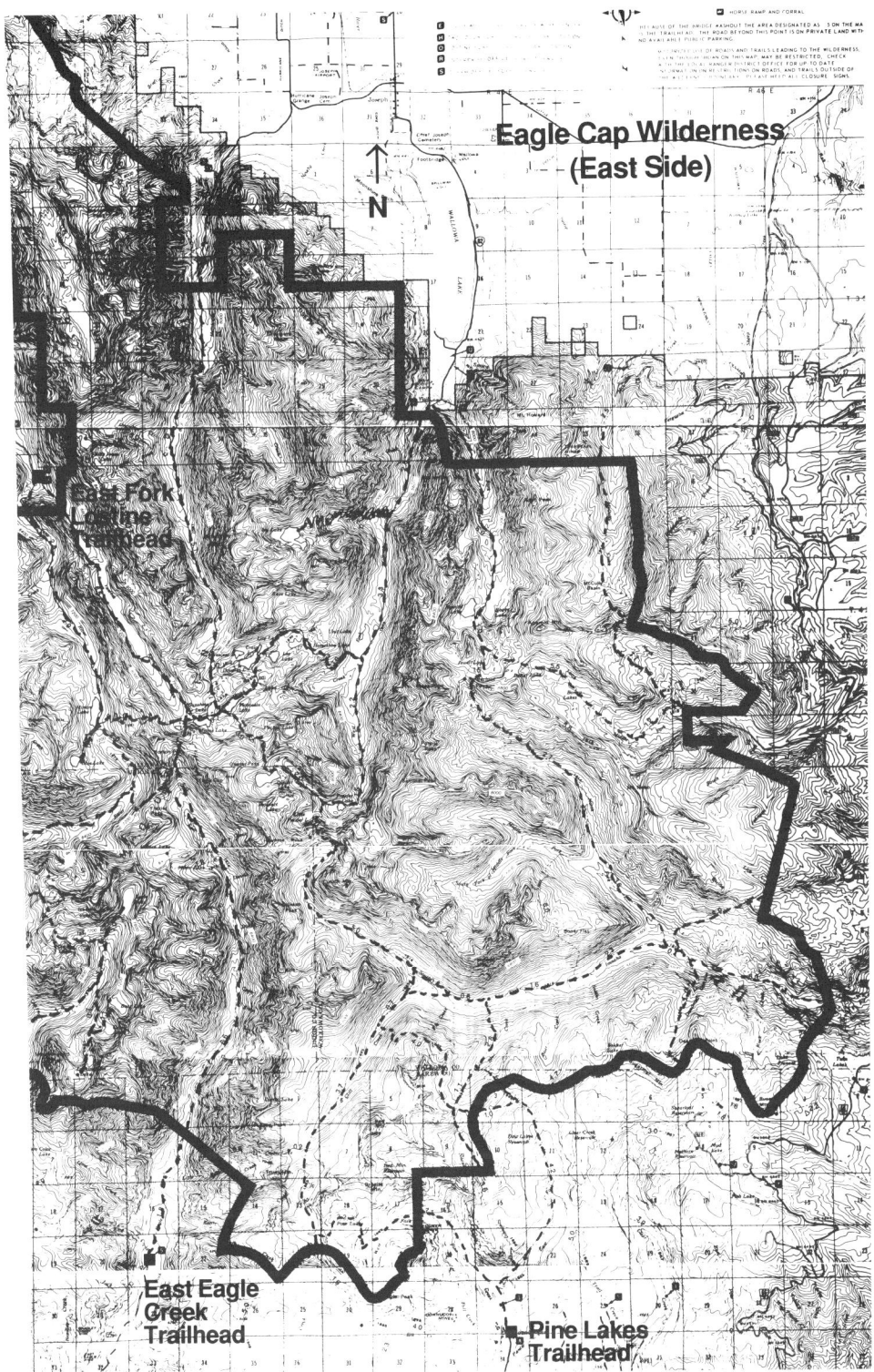

Traverse Lake

4 WEST EAGLE CREEK TRAILHEAD TO TRAVERSE LAKE

Distance: 7.3 miles (one-way)
Elevation gain: 2,240 feet; loss 50 feet
High Point: 7,760 feet
Usually open: July through October
Topographic map: Eagle Cap Wilderness Map
Obtain map from: Wallowa-Whitman National Forest

Hikers traveling from West Eagle Meadow to Traverse Lake will be rewarded for their efforts with magnificent views of the surrounding granite peaks. And in the proper season, wildflowers brighten up the trail as well. In addition, the fishing at Traverse Lake is good and a bonus for those carrying a fishing rod.

To reach the West Eagle Creek Trailhead drive Oregon Hwy. 203 south from the small town of Union where you can obtain supplies. Turn left onto FS Road No. 77 at 13.0 miles. A well-maintained gravel road for the first 10.0 miles, Road No. 77 turns into a rough dirt road after that. A sign recommends that passenger cars not attempt the trip.

Drive to West Eagle Meadow, 14.3 miles from Oregon Hwy. 203. Turn left, reaching the trailhead 0.3 mile down the road. There is plenty of parking at the trailhead with an outhouse nearby and camping for those who want to spend the night at the trailhead.

Begin an easy hike through the trees along West Eagle Creek Trail No. 1934 entering the Wilderness at 0.1 mile. A hundred feet farther reach the junction of Trail No. 1914. Continue up the easy trail, crossing the frigid waters of Fake Creek at 0.4 mile, and several other small streams during the easy up and down hike. At 0.8 mile cross West Eagle Creek via logs. At this point it appears that the trail continues on up the creek, but it doesn't. It's obvious, though, that many thought the same for there is a faint trail here. If you miss the turn the trail will suddenly grow very narrow as you're engulfed by vegetation.

Ford the creek or cross via some logs, picking up the trail on the other side, and crossing through a meadow soon after leaving the creek. At 1.5 miles begin moderate switchbacks along an open slope where you'll see many kinds of wildflowers during the summer months. At times, the switchbacks disappear as the trail climbs at a moderate grade, then reverts back to switchbacks.

At 2.1 miles there's a slight downhill to a creek (last chance for water for nearly three miles) at 2.2 miles. Cross the creek then begin a series of moderate switchbacks. At 2.8 miles reach the junction of Trail No. 1943 which heads left to Elk Creek. To reach Traverse Lake turn right. A sign reads right to "Trail Creek."

Continue up a long series of switchbacks, crossing an open slope with gorgeous views, reaching a fairly level spot and the fast-flowing waters of West Eagle Creek at 4.9 miles. Cross the creek following the easy trail to a small unnamed lake at 5.1 miles. Continue on up the moderate slope to several campsites in the trees at 5.5 miles. There's a stream near these sites as well.

Continue on to Echo Lake, a 28-acre lake stocked with eastern brook trout, at 5.6 miles. There is room to camp on the northeast end of the lake. From Echo Lake continue on up the trail, moderately climbing via switchback to a spring at 6.9 miles. From here, hike across the granite slopes to Traverse Lake at 7.3 miles. A huge granite peak appears to the east of the 31-acre lake which is also stocked with eastern brook trout. And at thirty-one feet deep, the lake is perfect for swimming.

5 MAIN EAGLE CREEK TRAILHEAD TO EAGLE LAKE

Distance: 7.4 miles (one-way)
Elevation gain: 2,529 feet; loss 120 feet
High point: 7,520 feet
Usually open: July through October
Topographic map: Eagle Cap Wilderness Map
Obtain map from: Wallowa-Whitman National Forest

Meadows, wildflowers, and a great view of Needlepoint Mountain are offered along this trail. If that isn't enough, the trail ends at magnificent Eagle Lake with granite peaks providing a nice backdrop to the deep blue waters of the lake. The fishing is good at Eagle Lake, and it is excellent swimming if you can stand the cold water.

To reach the Main Eagle Creek Trailhead at the old Boulder Park Resort, drive from Medical Springs (a small store is located at Pondosa just south of Medical Springs). Turn right at Medical Springs, heading south on Collins Road for 1.6 miles then left on FS Road No. 67. Drive 13.0 miles on Rd. No. 67 to the junction of FS Road No. 77. Turn left and continue up FS Road No. 77 to a fork at 0.7 mile. Turn right, driving FS Road No. 7755 for 3.7 miles to the trailhead.

There are plenty of campsites available off Road No. 7755 for those who would like to spend the night before or after their hike. Also, there is an old outhouse near the trailhead. For those who are wondering if Boulder Resort will reopen, the answer is no. The buildings at Boulder Resort will be removed sometime in the near future.

From the trailhead hike Main Eagle Creek Trail No. 1922, noticing the large rock slide on the right. The slide occurred in the spring of 1984, rushing down the mountainside and across the creek to Boulder Park. Remarkably, the creek bed was left boulder-free.

The trail heads through the trees then across Eagle Creek (via bridge) at 0.3 mile. Climb moderately from here, sometimes by switchback, then hike a gradual up and down through the trees to a small stream and the Wilderness Boundary at 1.5 miles.

Now the trail heads level or slightly downhill to another creek at 1.6 miles.

Cross a meadow soon after and another bridge at 2.3 miles. Look for a spur trail leading to a campsite in the trees to the right at 2.6 miles. Eagle Creek is near the camp and unless the creek water is extremely low, the fishing is usually good.

At 2.5 miles ford Copper Creek, looking for Copper Creek Falls (to the left) shortly thereafter. Continue up the moderate trail to a junction at 2.8 miles. To the left the trail heads to Bench Canyon. Stay right to reach Eagle Lake (sign reads "Trail Creek") climbing moderately through the mostly open area reaching a small stream at 3.0 miles.

Climb the moderate grade across the open/semi-open slope then head slightly downhill at 4.1 miles. Ahead lies a beautiful valley and a junction at 4.3 miles. The trail to the right leads to Lookingglass Lake (see #6, MAIN EAGLE CREEK TRAILHEAD TO LOOKINGGLASS LAKE), left to Eagle Lake (again, sign reads "Trail Creek"). There are several places to camp in this area and farther down the trail.

Stay straight, hiking gentle ups and downs to another stream at 4.7 miles. Climb moderately to 4.9 miles and a spur trail to another camp in the trees with Eagle Creek nearby. Climb moderately, sometimes hiking a slight downhill through the open then into the trees and across a creek at 5.4 miles. There are views of Needlepoint Mountain (9,032 feet) at various points along the trail now, especially as you near the slopes you'll soon be climbing.

Begin climbing moderate, sometimes steep switchbacks across an open slope at 5.9 miles. Reach a junction at 6.2 miles. Head right to Eagle Lake, which you will reach, at 7.4 miles.

All campsites are located at the south end of the lake because steep granite slopes surround most of the lake. At 104 feet deep, Eagle Lake is perfect for swimming, but only for those who can stand cold, cold water. Anglers will find plenty of eastern brook trout to hook, some up to 28 inches, and all visitors will find this 37-acre lake a pleasure to just sit and look at.

Eagle Lake

6 MAIN EAGLE CREEK TRAILHEAD TO LOOKINGGLASS LAKE

Distance: 7.4 miles (one-way)
Elevation gain: 2,369 feet; loss 240 feet
High point: 7,360 feet
Usually open: July through October
Topographic map: Eagle Cap Wilderness
Obtain map from: Wallowa-Whitman National Forest

This is one interesting hike along portions of Eagle Creek, through meadows and valleys, with great views of the granite slopes of Needlepoint Mountain. Lookingglass Lake is beautiful beyond words with a spectacular view looking once again towards Needlepoint Mountain. The fishing is good.

To reach Main Eagle Creek Trailhead, at the old Boulder Park Resort, drive from Medical Springs (a small store is located at Pondosa just south of Medical Springs). Turn right in Medical Springs heading south on Collins Road for 1.6 miles then left on FS Road No. 67. Drive 13.0 miles via Road 67 to the junction of FS Road No. 77. Turn left on Road No. 77, reaching a fork at 0.7 mile. Turn right, driving FS Road No. 7755 for 3.7 miles to the trailhead. There are plenty of areas to camp off Road No. 7755, with an outhouse located near the trailhead. Boulder Park Resort is no longer open and there are plans to remove the building sometime in the near future.

From the trailhead, hike Main Eagle Creek Trail No. 1922. Notice the huge slide to the right. The slide occurred in the spring of 1984, moving down the mountain, across the creek, and up to Boulder Resort. Remarkably, the creek bed remained open and free of boulders.

The trail heads through the trees now and across a bridge over Eagle Creek at 0.3 mile. Climb moderately from here, sometimes via switchback then a gradual up and down through the pines and dense vegetation. Cross a small stream entering the Wilderness at 1.5 miles. Gradually head level or slightly down to another creek at 1.6 miles.

Cross an open meadow and another bridge at 2.3 miles. At 2.6 miles look for a campsite in the trees to the right. A spur trail leads to the site which is located near Eagle Creek.

At 2.5 miles ford Copper Creek, keeping an eye open for Copper Creek Falls, a short ways down the trail and to the left. Continue up the trail to a junction at 2.8 miles. The trail to the left heads to Bench Canyon, stay to the right to reach Lookingglass Lake (sign reads "Trail Creek").

Climb the trail which leads across an open slope (sometimes semi-open), reaching a small stream at 3.0 miles, heading slightly downhill at 4.1 miles. Ahead lies a beautiful valley and a junction at 4.3 miles. The trail to the left leads to Eagle Lake. (See #5 MAIN EAGLE CREEK TRAILHEAD TO EAGLE LAKE for instructions.) The trail to the right leads to Lookingglass Lake.

Notice several campsites as you follow the trail to Eagle Creek. Ford the creek, then climb at a moderate (sometimes steep) grade through the trees with occasional breaks for a good view. At 5.3 miles reach a junction. Head right and up to Lookingglass Lake, leveling off at 5.5 miles and crossing a stream shortly thereafter. Continue up, climbing again across the open slope, crossing two streams at 6.3 miles and a couple more streams farther on.

Continue climbing, then level off, reaching a small pond and meadow, and your first view of Lookingglass Lake at 7.1 miles. Head down the moderate slope to Lookingglass Lake at 7.4 miles.

The view from Lookingglass is fantastic with Needlepoint Mountain and other granite peaks forming a spectacular backdrop. Campsites are limited due to the rocky and steep shore of this 31-acre lake. At 45 feet deep, Lookingglass Lake is perfect for swimming (although cold), and anglers can hook eastern brook, cutthroat, and brook trout.

Lookingglass Lake and Needlepoint Mountain

7 PINE LAKES TRAIL

Distance: 7.5 miles (one-way)
Elevation gain: 2,800 feet; loss 30 feet
High point: 7,600 feet
Usually open: July through October
Topographic map: Eagle Cap Wilderness Map
Obtain map from: Wallowa-Whitman National Forest

The trail to Pine Lakes offers splendid views and the chance to hike across talus slopes where pikas bark and chatter at others of their kind, running from rock to rock all the while. Then one can relax at either of the two scenic Pine Lakes.

To reach the trailhead at Cornucopia drive north from Halfway, Oregon, (gas and supplies available in town), heading north on Main and following the signs to Cornucopia. The road is paved for the first 5.3 miles then turns to gravel and is bumpy in sections. A sign warns "Road steep, windy, slippery when wet," but is passable with a passenger car. Reach a fork 10.3 miles from Halfway. Head right to the Cornucopia Pack Station 0.5 mile away. At the pack station the road forks, leading past an Eagle Cap Wilderness sign. Head left and park near another sign: "Pine Lakes - 7 miles."

Hike Pine Lakes Trail No. 1880 (a dirt road), then ford East Fork Creek at 0.2 mile. Ford another stream shortly thereafter, then follow the easy trail along the east side of West Pine Creek. Cross a bridge over West Pine Creek at 0.9 mile while admiring the view of Cornucopia Peak and Red Mountain. Continue up the trail which is mostly open with streamside vegetation, crossing another bridge over West Pine Creek at 1.9 miles.

Climb the semi-open slope, reaching a camp in the trees a few hundred yards from the creek. Continue up the moderate slope to a rock promontory and good view at 2.5 miles. From here switchback moderately across the open slope, entering the Wilderness at 3.4 miles. Continue on, crossing a talus slope then reaching a stream at 3.8 miles. Look for pikas and wrens in this area, then begin a series of moderate switchbacks to another stream at 4.8 miles.

The rocky trail heads nearly level now, and then passes through a grassy area before climbing up to a point where the trail edges back over and above the creek. Soon after, look for a waterfall on the north ridge. Pine Lakes is located above the falls.

At 5.5 miles the trail heads level or slightly downhill, passing through the trees and across a stream which is flowing from the falls. Climb the easy to moderate slope through an open meadow and begin switchbacks at 6.2 miles. Cross a couple of small springs while traversing up the hillside. Reach the smaller of the two Pine Lakes at 7.5 miles.

There are some good campsites in this area. Two are located as you hike the trail around the northeast side of the three-acre lake. Spur trails head off to the right at this point. Also, there is a site located between the two lakes.

The larger of the two Pine Lakes is located just to the west of the smaller one. There is camping on the south end of the 14-acre lake and one camp on the north end.

The lakes are excellent for swimming and fishing, ranging in depth from 35 to 70 feet deep. Both are stocked with eastern brook trout.

8 HIDDEN LAKE

Distance: 10.9 miles (one-way)
Elevation gain: 2,960 feet; loss 80 feet
High Point: 7,280 feet
Usually open: July through October
Topographic map: Eagle Cap Wilderness Map
Obtain map from: Wallowa-Whitman National Forest

It's a gradual climb up the East Eagle Creek drainage to the junction of Hidden Lake, but then the trail steepens. Once at Hidden Lake, though, you'll find it was well worth the climb.

To reach the East Eagle Creek Trailhead drive from Medical Springs (a small store is located in Pondosa just south of Medical Springs) via State Hwy. No. 203. Turn right (south) on Collins Road and take the paved road a short distance before it turns to gravel. Although bumpy at times, the road is in fairly good shape. Reach a fork at 1.6 miles. Head left on FS Road No. 67 to Eagle Creek. Reach a second fork after driving another 13.0 miles. Head right on FS Road No. 77 for 6.0 miles to FS Road No. 7745. (The Forest Service Map states that this is FS Road No. 7740. It is actually Road No. 7745.) Turn left, drive another 3.8 miles and park just before the sign: "Authorized Vehicles Only Beyond This Point."

This is not an actual trailhead. The trailhead is two miles down the road, but the bridge over East Eagle Creek washed out in 1977 and is currently (as of August 87) being rebuilt. Completion is expected during the summer of 1988. Also, a new road to the trailhead will be installed.

From the new trailhead you'll see Truax Mountain to the northeast and switchbacks heading up the slope to Crater Lake. Walk down the road reaching the area where the new bridge is being built at 0.5 mile. Cross Eagle Creek by fording the creek or crossing via a log then hike up the road at an easy grade. As you hike you'll see the sheer cliffs of Granite cliff to the north.

Continue to Little Kettle Trail No. 1945 at 1.9 miles. Crater Lake is 6.0 miles up the trail. Continue up the road reaching the old trailhead at 2.0 miles. A sign points the way to "Hidden Lake - 8.5 miles ahead." There is a large turnaround here and room to camp in the area as well.

Now the trail heads back near Eagle Creek and the confluence of Hudson Creek. Enter the Wilderness at 2.4 miles. Also, there is room to camp here or to park a vehicle as some have done. Pappy's Mine is also located in the area.

Now you're hiking a standard trail, sometimes across an open or semi-open slope, occasionally in old-growth forest. The trail heads up at a moderate grade then easy for the next few miles. Cross several dry streams before reaching a small stream at 4.2 miles. You'll find maiden hair fern here and ice-cold water. Cross Snow Creek at 4.4. miles then hike across the slope for a great view of Eagle Creek and the mountains to the north and northeast.

At 5.0 miles cross Coon Creek and at 6.0 miles reach a large flat area and a camp near Eagle Creek. Continue to 6.9 miles where you'll cross Dodge Creek. Just before reaching Dodge Creek notice the trail leading down the slope through the trees to another nice campsite, also near Eagle Creek.

Continue through the meadow dotted with flowers, a few trees, and great views of the East Eagle Creek drainage for most of the hike. At 7.2 miles cross another creek.

There's a long, flat area and a spot to camp at 8.0 miles. There are boulders to the right, prime habitat for the endearing pika. Continue through the meadow to an unsigned junction at 9.0 miles. There is a post here, but the sign is missing. Ford East Eagle Creek then head up the steep slope. There's a camp in the trees to the left at 9.1 miles and another camp to the right in the trees at 9.4 miles.

Continue the steep climb until the trail levels off near Moon Lake at 10.4 miles. There's room to camp at Moon Lake, but Hidden Lakes is the most spectacular and it's obvious that most people camp there. Continue around the north end of the lake, climbing the steep ridge, then down the moderate to steep trail to a small stream at 10.9 miles. Cross the stream, hike 200 yards to the northwest, and look for campsites on the north, south, and west ends of 16-acre Hidden Lake. Those with a yearning for fish will find tasty eastern brook trout in this scenic lake.

Looking east from Hidden Lake

9 JIM WHITE RIDGE LOOP

Distance: 21.4 miles (complete loop)
Elevation gain: 3,480 feet; loss 3,480 feet
High point: 7,440 feet
Usually open: July through October
Topographic map: Eagle Cap Wilderness Map
Obtain map from: Wallowa-Whitman National Forest

This loop is particularly nice because crowds are few and far between, and there are good views into the Little Minam River drainage, the Minam River drainage, and to the east there are the high peaks of the Eagle Cap Mountains. Also, there's the chance of seeing grouse, deer, elk, squirrels, hawks, and golden eagles.

To reach the Moss Spring Trailhead, drive to Cove, Oregon, a small town offering gas and supplies, located 16 miles east of La Grande. Turn east off Oregon Hwy. 237 at the sign "Moss Springs CG." The paved road turns to gravel at 3.0 miles. Although it isn't signed, the road you're now traveling is FS Road No. 6220. Continue on, coming to a fork another 0.3 mile down the road. Head right, driving 5.0 miles to a fork and the entrance to Moss Spring Campground. Turn right and drive through the campground to the trailhead 0.2 mile away.

Begin hiking at the Moss Spring Trailhead sign, heading east, and reach a fork 100 yards down the trail. Little Minam River is to the right, Minam River to the left. Head to the right (counter-clockwise) for the easiest loop which will end by hiking the trail to the left. Please note, those hiking the loop in a clockwise direction will find many steep sections of trail to negotiate.

Hike down the easy to moderate trail through the trees, then switchback down to Fireline Creek at 1.2 miles. Now the trail is level. Continue to the unsigned junction of Trail No. 1913 at 2.0 miles. Head straight, crossing a creek in 100 feet, then continue to the Little Minam River, another 100 yards to the north. There is a campsite here, but shouldn't be used as it is too close to the river. Cross the river and begin an easy to moderate climb across the tree-covered slope.

Cross streams at 2.7 miles and again at 2.9 and 4.0 miles. Now head out onto an open slope, crossing another stream at 4.2 miles. The trail passes through the trees, and across both semi-open and open slopes now, with a series of switchbacks beginning at 4.7 miles. Reach another stream at 5.0 miles and another shortly thereafter.

Continue up the slope passing through a burned-out area. Come to two more streams at 6.1 miles and 6.5 miles and notice the view to the west. Reach another stream at 6.9 miles. Continue up the easy to moderate slope to a junction at 7.8 miles. Rock Creek Trail heads to the east, hike north to Jim White Ridge.

Climb the moderate slope then level off for a fantastic view of the Wilderness to the east and beyond. Now descend the easy slope to an unsigned junction at 8.2 miles. The unmaintained trail to the right leads to water at Pot Creek in addition to several nice campsites. Although the 0.4 mile trail isn't maintained by the Forest Service, it is in fairly good condition, dropping 320 feet to water and one of the nicest spots for camping along the whole loop. (It's possible to camp on the ridge, but flat sites are almost nonexistent, the ground is rocky, and there isn't any water.)

From the junction at Pot Creek the trail gradually heads up and down or level in some sections. Reach the junction of Little Pot Creek Trail No. 1919 at 8.9 miles. Shortly thereafter come to a fork. Head to the right, following the rock cairns up the ridge. It's easy to turn left at this junction for the trail to the left is worn from heavy use. It does not lead to Jim White Ridge, however. Instead it heads down Young Ridge via the Salt Trail, an old sheep herders trail. This trail leads to the Little Minam River, but it is not a designated trail and is not maintained by the Forest Service.

Back on the ridge, follow the rock cairns, and find a small trail after the last cairn. Follow it to the right heading across a saddle to Jim White Ridge. The trail primarily heads down now, descending at an easy to moderate grade, but does climb up in short sections. The trail runs across the open slope, into the trees, then out onto an open slope again at 10.6 miles.

Now the trail heads up, climbing at a steep grade to a high point and wonderful view. Head across the ridge, then begin hiking down to the tree-covered trail at 11.1 miles. The trail heads to the right and isn't too obvious in places so follow the blazed trees. The trail curves back to the north then descends at a steep grade with some switchbacks at 11.5 miles.

Reach a stream at 15.8 miles. There is a camp located about 100 feet down the trail. Continue to another stream crossing at 16.0 miles. Reach the junction of the Minam River Trail and Moss Spring Trail No. 1908 at 17.0 miles. Head straight 100 yards and across the bridge over Little Minam River. Before crossing the river you'll find camps located here and on the west side of the river, about 100 yards after crossing the bridge.

The trail heads up at an easy to moderate grade, through the trees, with an occasional slight descent now and then. There are many small streams to cross and a campsite near the river at 19.2 miles.

At 20.1 miles cross a bridge over Horseshoe Creek and head away from the Little Minam River. At 20.8 miles the trail climbs at a steep angle across an open slope for a while then back into the trees. Reach the trailhead at 21.4 miles.

10 SWAMP LAKE/ STEAMBOAT LAKE/ JOHN HENRY LAKE LOOP

Distance: 31.5 miles (complete loop)
Elevation gain: 6,060 feet; loss 6,060 feet
High point: 8,560 feet
Usually open: July through October
Topographic map: Eagle Cap Wilderness Map
Obtain map from: Wallowa-Whitman National Forest

This loop is more popular than some of the wilderness trails mentioned in this guidebook, but not nearly as crowded as the Lakes Basin Loop which we avoided. (See INTRODUCTION TO THE EAGLE CAP WILDERNESS for more information regarding the Lakes Basin.) The loop passes a variety of deep blue lakes and weaves through the West Fork Lostine River and the North Minam River drainages. As in most sections of the Wilderness, there are spectacular views of the surrounding area.

To reach the trailhead drive Oregon Hwy. 82 to Lostine, Oregon, a small town with supplies and gasoline. Head south at the sign "Lostine River Campgrounds." The paved road turns to gravel at 7.0 miles. Now FS Road No. 8210 is a rough, bumpy road, leading to the Bowman Trailhead another 8.0 miles up the road. Begin the loop here or at the East Fork Lostine Trailhead 3.8 miles farther. There is plenty of parking at both trailheads, especially the East Fork Lostine Trailhead where the following guide begins.

Start at the trailhead which leads to both East Fork Lostine Trail No. 1662 and Minam Lake Trail No. 1670. Head through the trees, reaching a junction and the Wilderness boundary at 0.1 mile. Stay right, hiking Minam Lake Trail No. 1670. It's a moderate grade to a cement bridge over the East Fork Lostine River at 0.3 mile then the trail heads back near the West Fork Lostine River at 1.1 miles. Notice the waterfall across the river.

The trail is easy to moderate now with an occasional steep section. Level off at 2.0 miles then climb moderately through the trees to 2.6 miles. There's a log across the river here and a nice spot to camp on the opposite side.

From this point continue to a junction at 2.8 miles. Head right via Trail No. 1656 towards Copper Creek. There is room to camp on the left as you pass the meadow on the right. Then ford the East Fork Lostine a couple hundred yards ahead.

Climb the easy to moderate trail. At 3.7 miles begin a slight downhill. There's a camp on the left side at this point. Ford scenic Copper Creek about 200 feet down the trail from the camp.

At 4.5 miles there are some easy ups and downs and a good view of Elkhorn Peak to the northwest. Reach another creek at 4.6 miles and another camp in the trees just before fording the creek.

Now the trail heads through an open meadow at a level grade then climbs again at 5.0 miles. Switchback up the slope to 5.7 miles and a small stream. The trail is fairly level once again, crossing another stream at 5.9 miles.

Head up the open slope reaching an ice-cold spring at 6.4 miles. Next the easy to moderate trail leads to a large sandy area at 7.3 miles. From here there is a grand view of the 9,832 foot Matterhorn, and 9,839 foot Sacajawea Peak to the northeast, and Eagle Cap, at 9,595 feet, to the southeast.

Continue hiking at a level to downhill grade to a junction at 7.8 miles, taking in the spectacular view of Swamp Lake to the north. To the left, Trail No. 1676 heads down to the Minam River. Take the right fork, Trail No. 1675, towards the North Minam River.

It's an easy down across the open slope, hiking a series of moderate switchbacks at 8.4 miles. Reach a spring at 9.0 miles and a camp nearby. Continue down to level ground and a bridge at 9.2 miles.

At 9.7 miles reach the north end of Swamp Lake where you'll find room to camp and the junction to Long Lake, via Trail No. 1669. Keep on the trail to the right and head up the slope to the top of the ridge and a wonderful view of Steamboat Lake at 10.1 miles.

Hike moderate switchbacks across the mostly open slope, watching for pikas as you descend. Reach level ground and ford a stream at 11.0 miles. Remain on the trail to a point where the trail heads up again. You'll find a camp at 11.5 miles. This camp, and several others, are located near the center of the east side of the lake.

Moderately climb up the slope to 11.7 miles then begin an easy down, crossing a couple of streams at 11.8 miles. Now it's an easy up and down, crossing several more streams while hiking through the meadows. At 12.8 miles there is a good view of the North Minam River Basin. Switchback down the semi-open slope crossing several streams as you descend to the trees at 15.5 miles. Reach the North Minam River at 16.9 miles then follow the trail as it winds along the outskirts of North Minam Meadow to your left. Reach the junction of Wilson Basin at 17.4 miles. (There are numerous campsites from the 16.5 miles mark to the Wilson Basin Junction with water at the river.)

Turn right, hiking Bowman Trail No. 1651, and climbing the moderate switchbacks across the semi-open slope. Enter the trees at 18.8 miles. Continue to 19.9 miles where the trail crosses the creek via logs. There are campsites to the right with a view of the nearby meadow and Lookout Mountain to the north.

It's an easy hike to the junction of Bear Creek at 20.0 miles. Continue across the semi-open slope to 20.8 miles and an abundance of fallen trees, knocked down by a January 1986 avalanche.

Head into the trees, crossing a small stream at 21.0 miles. Reach the unsigned junction to John Henry Lake at 21.2 miles. This trail is not maintained by the Forest Service and was originally made by horse people who frequent the area. Follow the trail to where it peters out, cross the meadow, and continue on the well-defined trail near some fallen trees. There's a camp near the junction just before crossing the meadow. Follow the easy trail through the trees, passing a couple of camps and another lake before reaching John Henry Lake at 21.6 miles.

There are plenty of campsites at John Henry Lake. At least two are located on the east side and a few more as you head around to the west side of the lake.

To complete the loop, head back to the junction at 22.0 miles. Head up the forested slope via switchback then out onto a semi-open slope. The climb is moderate. Reach the top of the ridge at 23.2 miles. A wonderful spot for lunch or a break, there is a splendid view to the west, and to the east see Twin Peaks and Bowman Creek.

Switchback down the easy to moderate slope to a junction at 24.1 miles. Chimney Lake is to your left, Lostine Canyon straight ahead. Stay straight, eventually hiking through the trees, crossing Bowman Creek at the 24.8 and 26.2 miles mark.

Reach Bowman Creek again at 26.9 miles and for the last time at 27.5 miles. Cross via the bridge or ford the creek using the path to your right. Stay straight and reach a wilderness boundary sign at 27.6 miles. Hike across the bridge over the Lostine River just before reaching the Bowman Creek Trailhead at 27.7 miles.

Now it's an easy hike up the road 3.8 miles to the trailhead at East Fork Lostine, a total loop of 31.5 miles.

Along trail from Steamboat Lake to North Minam River

Old mowing machine near McGraw Cabin

INTRODUCTION TO THE HELLS CANYON WILDERNESS

Hells Canyon! It's the deepest gorge in North America, and according to the 1987 Guinness Book of World Records, it's "the deepest canyon in low relief territory."

From atop Seven Devils Mountain in Idaho, Hells Canyon plunges an amazing 7,900 feet to the mighty Snake River. In between the high mountains and low-lying river there's a world of steep cliffs and bunchgrass plateaus. It's a place where elk, deer, bear, mountain goats, mountain lion, and bighorn sheep roam. A place where eagles soar on high, and falcons dive on unsuspecting prey.

Set apart from the nine other areas listed in this guidebook, Hells Canyon Wilderness is unusual in that it is included as part of a larger protected area, the Hells Canyon National Recreation Area (NRA).

Established by Congress on December 31, 1975, Hells Canyon NRA straddles the Hells Canyon of the Snake River, stretching west to the mountain slopes of northeast Oregon, and east to the peaks of west central Idaho's Seven Devils Mountains.

Hells Canyon NRA consists of a total of 652,488 acres, 216,832 acres of which have been designated Hells Canyon Wilderness. Much of the current Wilderness was designated as such when Congress established the NRA in December of 1975. Additional acreage, however, was added with the passage of the Oregon Wilderness Act of 1984.

As mentioned previously, the Wilderness blankets a portion of two states, 127,000 acres of which are located in Oregon, 84,800 in Idaho. (Because this book deals with those Wilderness Areas found in eastern Oregon, Idaho's trails were not traveled.)

Hells Canyon was designated wilderness for several reasons. According to Alan Defler, Project Manager at NRA, "the original classification movement began as an effort to stop further dam construction on the Snake River." Defler also adds, "acreage was added to preserve the unique characteristics of the canyon itself."

Unique characteristics include an abundance of prehistoric and historic sites, as well as several threatened or endangered wildlife and plant species. These species include the peregrine falcon, bald eagle, Barton berry, and lovely penstemon.

The Wallowa-Whitman National Forest manages both the NRA and Wilderness, and maintains (some annually, some not so often) nearly 1,000 miles of trail which penetrate the area, 352 miles of which lead into the Wilderness. Approximately 210 miles traverse Oregon's side, 142 miles on Idaho's side.

Three National Recreation Trails and one National Historic Trail traverse the NRA. The Nee-Me-Poo Trail, a National Historic Trail, is found on the Oregon side and is included in this guidebook. Although two of the National Recreation Trails lie in Idaho, one, the Western Rim National Recreation Trail, is located in Oregon. The Western Rim Trail extends 40 miles, from the P.O. Saddle north to Dug Bar. Skirting the western rim of the Snake River Canyon, portions of this route are open to 4-wheel drive vehicles. (Of course, these portions are located in the NRA, not in the Wilderness.) Sections of the Western Rim Trail are also included in this guide.

Trails lead across side canyons, over grassy benchlands, through timbered ridgetops, and down to the Snake River. Although the Snake River is not included as part of the Hells Canyon Wilderness, it is designated as a Wild and Scenic River. The Wild and Scenic portion of the river extends 31.5 river miles, from Hells Canyon Dam to Pittsburg Landing. From the dam to Johnson Bar, a total of 17 miles, the canyon walls are exceptionally steep and the river is at its best, for some of the largest white water rapids in all of North America are located here.

One of the larger rivers in the United States, the Snake begins life on the western slopes of the Continental Divide in Yellowstone National Park, Wyoming, and flows 1,000 miles to join the Columbia River near Pasco, Washington. The Snake is the largest tributary of the Columbia River, a scenic river border dividing the two states of Oregon and Washington.

At the opposite end of the scale is Hat Point, a popular point at 6,982 feet where one can gaze down at the Snake River, winding along some 1,276 feet above sea level. Averaging about 10 miles from rim to rim, the canyon is between five and six thousand feet deep in some places.

Visitors will find portions of Hells Canyon accessible year-round. The Forest Service, though, recommends spring, late summer and early fall, as the best times for backpacking. Those that crave few crowds and uncrowded camp areas, however, should avoid hiking into Hells Canyon in October for the area is alive with deer and elk hunters.

Daytime temperatures during the summer months average 90 degrees and water can be quite scarce so enter the area fully prepared. Spring and fall are cooler, a bonus for avid backpackers.

Because of the great diversity in elevation, visitors will encounter several different climatic zones. Mild winters and hot summers are encountered at the low elevation areas, with cool summers and severe winters at higher elevations. Those wanting to visit during the winter season will usually find relatively mild temperatures along the Snake River, with a little snow blanketing the ground some years.

Several trailheads provide year-round access to the area. These include Dug Bar, Cow Creek, and Freezeout. Warnock Corrals and P.O. Saddle, however, are only open during summer and early fall. Please note that most roads leading to the trailheads are narrow dirt roads, sometimes impassable during spring months. (We visited Hells Canyon during May, 1988, a particularly dry year, but we were not able to get to some of the trailheads we had planned to hike from. Because of a thick blanket of snow on some roads, we spent more time in the northern and southern portions of the Wilderness. Those entering the area during the summer and fall may want to hike from Warnock Corrals down Temperance Creek, a hike we heard is very nice. Be prepared to ford the creek many times, however. One horseback rider told us he counted 21 or 22 crossings.)

Plant species are as varied as the terrain. At the lowest altitudes, shrubs and grasses are predominant with an occasional ponderosa pine found on exposed streamsides. White alder, box elder, and water birch are common along streamsides.

Farther up the slopes there is a variety of bunchgrass species, and often cheatgrass is found on overgrazed slopes. Above 4,000 feet you'll find dense stands, especially on the moist north slopes, of Douglas-fir with some ponderosa and ninebark pine. Grand fir and subalpine fir associations are generally found above 5,000 feet.

Wildlife abounds in such conditions. A total of 347 species of animal life live within the NRA. These include: ten amphibians, 12 reptiles, 249 birds, and 76 mammals. Our nation's symbol, the American bald eagle, is found in small numbers along the Snake River during the winter, particularly along Hells Canyon Reservoir. The endangered peregrine falcon is also occasionally sighted. Animals listed as threatened or as a species of special concern include the spotted frog, wolverine, snowy plover, ferruginous hawk, mountain quail, fisher, and bobcat.

Rocky Mountain elk are native to the area and are thriving (elk seem to be everywhere we looked during the early morning and late evening hours), although during the late 1800's their numbers were drastically reduced. Elk transplanted from the Yellowstone area and restrictive hunting regulations, however, have assisted in their recovery. A 1981 State of Oregon survey shows 4,000 elk now live in the area between the Snake and Imnaha River drainages.

Mule deer are also found in the area. Rocky Mountain bighorn sheep were reintroduced near Battle Creek and along Summit Ridge where they live in their preferred habitat, steep and rocky cliffs. Other mammals found in Hells Canyon include mountain goats, black bear, mountain lion, marmots, squirrels, badger, wolverines, pine marten, and fisher.

Bird life includes a variety of small game species of which chukar partridge is the most sought after. Other popular birds include gray partridge, California and mountain quail, and blue, ruffed, and Franklin grouse. Franklin grouse is considered unique and is protected in Oregon where it is found in high elevation pine and fir thickets.

Old-growth habitat provides the necessary conditions for the barred owl. Other bird species found in the area, besides the falcons and eagles mentioned earlier, include the golden eagle and prairie falcon. Waterfowl such as the cliff dwelling Canada goose, mallard and Barrows goldeneye ducks are common along the Snake River.

Hikers will want to keep especially alert when hiking in Hells Canyon for there are rattlesnakes and black widow spiders. As a matter of precaution, the Forest Service advises carrying a snake bite kit. Poison oak is something else you'll want to avoid. Look for this shiny, three-leaved plant along the lower reaches of Hells Canyon, especially along the Snake River, and lower creek drainages.

While rich in wildlife, Hells Canyon is also rich in history. The famous Lewis and Clark Expedition of 1805 found the Nez Perce Indians the primary occupants of Hells Canyon. Also, the Nez Perce lived in the Wallowa Valley and what came to be called the Imnaha Valley. Shoshone-Bannock, Northern Paiute and Cayuse Indians were also frequent visitors of Hells Canyon.

With the arrival of the white man and discovery of gold the Indians were forced off their land, a move which resulted in the famous Nez Perce War of 1877.

Once the Indians were removed from their land, white settlers began grazing domestic livestock, and by the year 1880 white settlement of the remote and rugged country known as Hells Canyon and the Imnaha valley had begun.

During the late 1800's and the early 1900's, numerous homesteads were developed on the benchland of Oregon and near the mouths of major streams along the Snake River. Today, there are 35 acres of private land within the Wilderness and sheep and cattle graze within the area too.

Homesteading was described in a variety of ways by local residents. One individual claimed, "The Government bet you 160 acres that you couldn't live there three years without starving to death." For years, folks have claimed that, "It has never been easy to get around in Hells Canyon." But homesteaders found the mild climate in Imnaha valley more than adequate for wintering livestock and for raising fruits and vegetables.

Much of Hells Canyon's history was made by those with the yearning to discover riches in the form of gold and copper. Gold was first reported in February of 1860, and by the following year there were placer mines at both ends of Hells Canyon, but miners found that searching for gold was, for the most part anyway, unprofitable.

A wide variety of fish inhabit the streams and rivers that flow through the Wilderness. America's largest freshwater fish, the white sturgeon, lurks beneath the blue waters of the Snake River. Because they are low in numbers, if you hook one of these giants you will have to return it to the river.

In addition to white sturgeon, there are warm water sportfish such as black crappie, smallmouth bass and channel catfish, and rough fish like coarse-scale suckers and squawfish. The Snake River system continues to support important runs of chinook salmon and steelhead trout. Kokanee salmon are also present.

When some folks think of Hells Canyon and the Snake River, they think of outdoor enthusiasts rafting down busy rapids. While rafting is certainly a favorite outdoor activity, some choose to ride the river via jet boat, others day hike, and still others decide to backpack. Also, there are those who come to hunt, fish, photograph, or ride horseback, and while they come for various reasons, they all have one thing in common. They came to experience Hells Canyon Wilderness.

For more information contact:

Wallowa-Whitman National Forest
P.O. Box 907
Baker, OR 97814
(503) 423-6391

or

Hells Canyon National Recreation Area
P.O. Box 490
Enterprise, OR 97828
(503) 426-3151

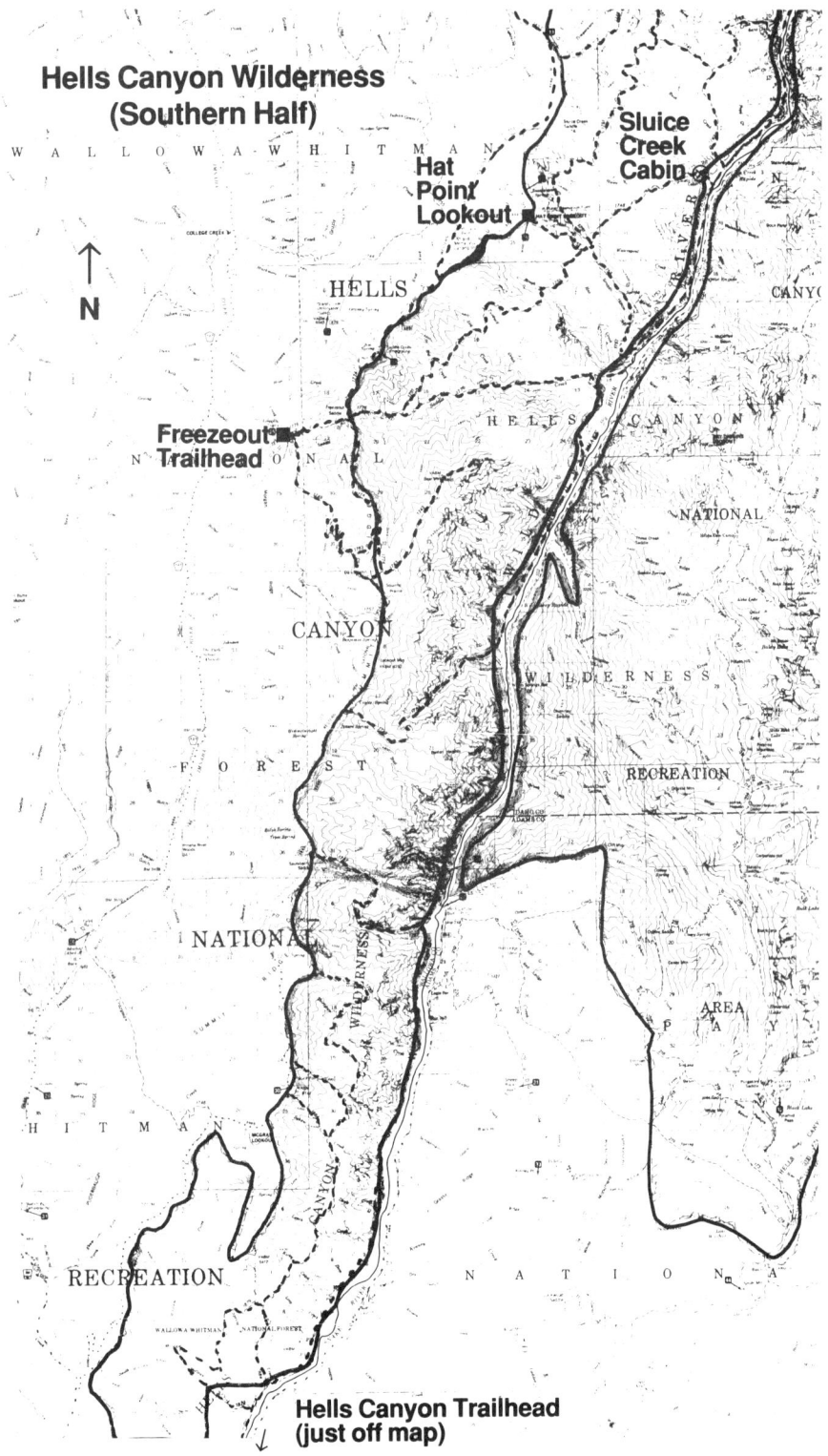

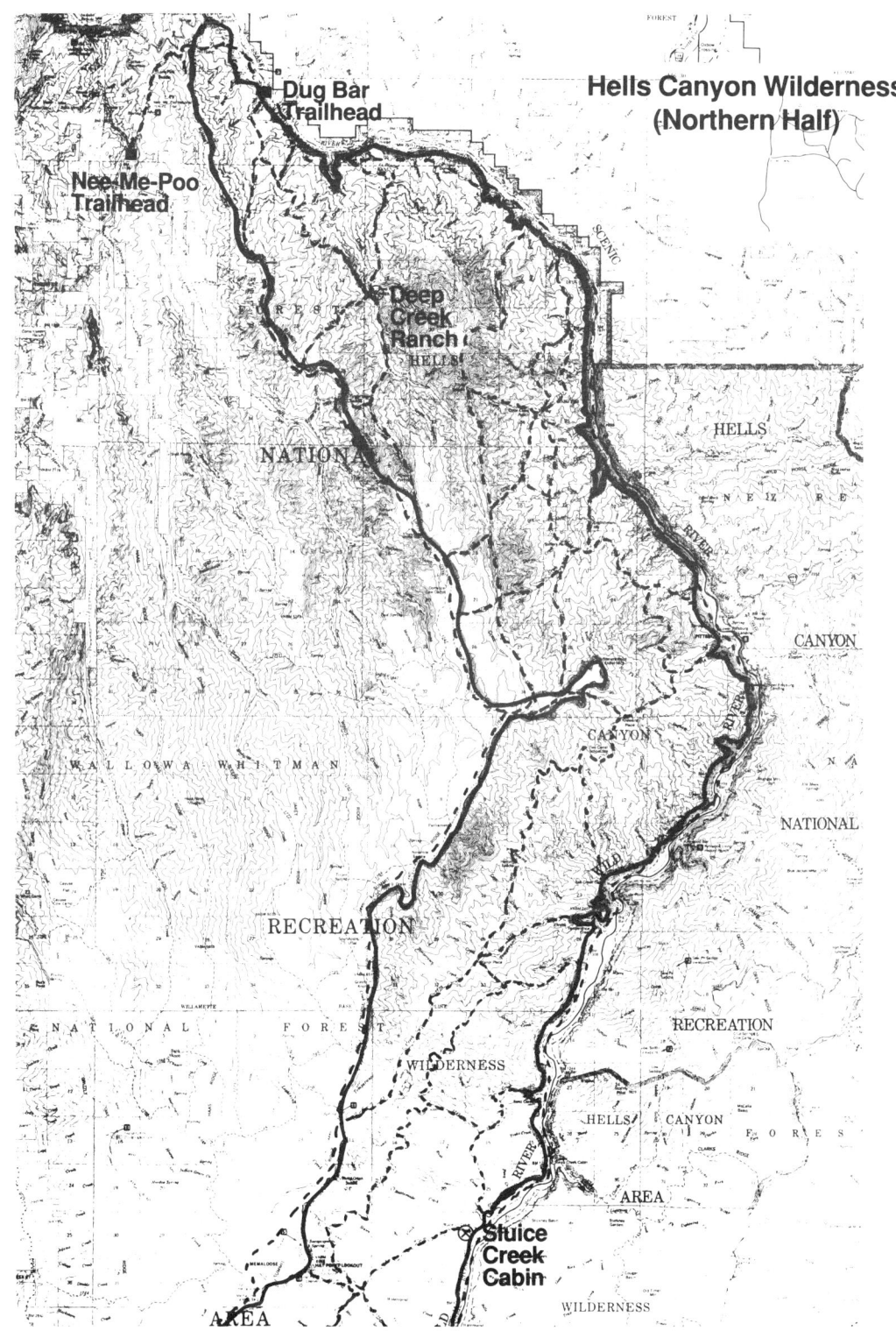

11 MCGRAW CABIN LOOP

Distance: 14.2 miles (complete loop)
Elevation gain: 2,260 feet; loss 2,260 feet
High point: 3,360 feet
Usually open: All year, but does occasionally close due to snow
Topographic map: Hells Canyon Wilderness Map
Obtain map from: Hells Canyon NRA Headquarters or Wallowa-Whitman National Forest

This trail is especially good in the spring when wildflowers blanket many of the upper slopes and all surrounding slopes are tinged light green. Those allergic to poison oak should note that the plant is found at the lower portions of both Spring and McGraw Creeks, also along the Snake River.

There are two ways of reaching Hells Canyon Trailhead, one from Baker, Oregon, the other from Joseph, Oregon. (Both towns have gas, food, and hiking supplies.) To reach the trailhead from Baker, drive Oregon Hwy. 86 east for 70.0 miles. Turn left on County Road No. 1039, a dirt road, and head past the sign leading to "Hells Canyon Trail." Reach the end of the road in 9.0 miles.

To reach the trailhead from Joseph, drive Wallowa Road from town (towards Imnaha), to the junction of Cloverdale Road at 8.3 miles. After 5.0 miles the road enters Forest Service land and becomes FS Road No. 39. All but 5 miles of the road is paved, the remaining 5 miles of gravel due to be paved during the summer of 1988. Drive this to the junction of Oregon Hwy. 86, another 49.0 miles away. Turn left, reaching County Road No. 1039 in 7.2 miles. Proceed to the end of the road as mentioned above.

There is little room to park at the trailhead, although there shouldn't be a problem finding a spot for a couple of vehicles. Enter near what appears to be an old Forest Service sign, then head north via Hells Canyon Trail No. 1890 and descend to Copper Creek in 100 yards.

The trail now climbs up and down gradually, following along the lower reaches of the Snake River Canyon, reaching Nelson Creek at 1.1 miles. Along the way, you'll always have a great view of the Snake River, also the opportunity to see lots of fish (it's the largest quantity of fish we've ever seen). In addition, there are kingfishers to enchant each hiker, an occasional raven, and more.

Ford Nelson Creek then continue on to McGraw Creek and a bridge at 2.1 miles. This is a nice spot for camping. Continue on the Bench Trail or hike the loop in reverse by climbing up McGraw Creek Trail No. 1879 and descending Bench Trail No. 1884. Although either would be nice, this loop heads up Bench Trail and down McGraw Creek Trail.

Continue north from McGraw Creek and reach a Forest Service boundary sign at 2.8 miles. Now you are in Hells Canyon National Recreation Area. At 2.9 miles reach the junction to Bench Trail No. 1884.

Climb up the slope then down to the south side of Spring Creek. Climb gradually now, mostly through the trees, crossing the creek a couple of times before the final crossing of Spring Creek at 3.8 miles. Follow the trail to the right, past a fallen sign, then head north. Now the trail leads across open slopes, through drainages, and is somewhat difficult to follow because vegetation has grown over the trail. Look for an occasional rock cairn which should prove a big help.

At 4.0 miles cross a dry drainage and turn left. Now the trail follows the drainage then heads up and across a small stream at 4.3 miles. As you hike, listen and look for chukars which seem to be everywhere.

Head up the ridge to the left about 100 yards past the creek. Continue northeast along the ridge then begin a series of steep switchbacks at 4.8 miles. In the spring, abundant wildflowers carpet the way, making the trip up the slope a real treat. Reach a junction and sign at 5.6 miles.

McGraw Cabin Trail No. 1879 is located just before the sign and descends at a rather steep grade down another flower-covered slope. Reach a small stream at 5.9 miles.

Now the trail is level or a slight up and down to 6.4 miles then a steep descent to Spring Creek at 6.7 miles. Look for elk in this area and across on the nearby slopes.

Continue on, hiking up and down to a large flat area at 7.4 miles. A nice stand of ponderosa pine trees shade the area with many good sites for dry camping. Spring Creek is the nearest creek. (This portion of the hike and a portion nearer to McGraw

Cabin are located on private land although neither area is occupied.)

From the giant ponderosas, hike south-southeast, passing between a group of several trees before rounding a bend. Now the trail heads west and down to a broken-down fence at 8.6 miles. Head across another flat area now, passing an old mowing machine on the way. At 8.9 miles begin a moderate decent to McGraw Cabin at 9.3 miles.

Dan Perkins, his wife, and three of his six children, visited the cabin on June 26, 1984 and left a note explaining their reason for hiking up to the cabin. Perkins first came to the area 51 years ago as a 10-day old baby. His parents, Luther and Blanche Perkins, rode up McGraw creek and found this hunk of land which they homesteaded and built the cabin. They had a garden, orchard, and an alfalfa field where the old mowing machine is located. The Forest Service also claims that at one time Perkins supposedly raised turkeys on his land, herding them down to Baker at sale time.

After exploring the cabin, do not take the trail to the creek. Instead, head to the left of the fence and to the left of the trail to the creek. Hike a gradual to moderate grade on the north side of the creek. Ford the creek at 10.1 miles.

It's a beautiful hike through the McGraw Creek drainage. There are pines, dense vegetation, and rugged cliffs high above the creek. Gradually descend to another creek crossing at 10.5 miles, another at 10.7 miles, and yet another 100 feet from the last. All crossings are made without a bridge.

Soon after the last crossing the descent is made across a mostly open slope and descends at a moderate to steep grade. Reach the junction of the Hells Canyon Trail at 12.1 miles. Turn right and continue back to the trailhead, completing the loop at 14.2 miles.

Canadian goose

12 NEE-ME-POO TRAIL

Distance: 4.3 miles (one-way)
Elevation gain: 840 feet; loss 1,640 feet
High point: 2,640 feet
Usually open: At least 10 months of the year, sometimes year-round, depending on the amount of snow.
Topographic map: Hells Canyon Wilderness Map
Obtain map from: Hells Canyon National Recreation Area or Wallowa-Whitman National Forest

The Wallowa Valley was home to the Nez Perce Indians and their ancestors for countless generations, but in the spring of 1877 General Howard of the U.S. Army ordered the Indians onto a reservation in Idaho. The influx of settlers, cattlemen, and gold miners was forcing the Indians to move elsewhere.

Reluctantly Chief Joseph and his band of 400 Indians, including about 64 braves, headed east to the Snake River, taking over 1,000 head of horses and cattle, but leaving much of their stock behind. The Nee-Me-Poo National Recreation Trail was but a small portion of the route they followed to the Snake, crossing at Dug Bar where a sign explains the events of that time.

After crossing the Snake River, Chief Joseph's band of Nez Perce joined other bands of Nez Perce and a small group of Palouses. Soon after, the historical Nez Perce War began as the Indians fled to Canada where they hoped to find freedom. Their journey covered about 1,800 miles as they headed north, confusing and outwitting 2,000 regular troops of the U.S. Army. Burdened with small children, women, and the elderly throughout their journey, the Nez Perce were able to outdistance the troops until they reached the Bear Paw Mountains of Montana, just 30 miles from the Canadian border. It was there, so close to freedom, that the Nez Perce were forced to surrender.

To reach the historic Nee-Me-Poo Trail, drive Wallowa Road east from Joseph, Oregon, for 30 miles to the small town of Imnaha. Here you'll find a cafe, gas, and a store. Turn left (north) on paved Lower Imnaha Road and follow this to FS Road No. 4260 at 6.5 miles. The road to the Nee-Me-Poo Trail and Dug Bar is somewhat rocky, narrow, and steep. It is also slippery when wet and 4-wheel drive is recommended for traveling under those conditions. Trailers are not recommended, but passenger cars can reach the trailhead if they negotiate the last 10 miles carefully and can climb steep grades.

After 1.6 miles enter Hells Canyon NRA and another 11.9 miles down the road cross a bridge, the Imnaha River is now on the west side of the road. Continue 2.8 miles to the Nee-Me-Poo National Historic Trailhead. There's room for a vehicle to park here, or better yet, have someone drive to the opposite end of the trail at Dug Bar and pick you up there. To reach Dug Bar by road continue another 7.8 miles.

Back at the western end of the trail, a sign points the way to Lone Pine Saddle. Head up the open slope, looking for prickly pear cactus along the way. Those hiking the trail in the spring may see the cactus in bloom. The trail climbs gradual to moderate, occasionally dipping into a small drainage then back up the other side. At 0.9 mile cross a fence and cross another fence just before reaching Lone Pine Saddle at 1.2 miles. There's a great view from here, but you can't see the Snake River.

Descend around a series of slopes now, reaching Big Canyon Creek at 2.2 miles. Big Canyon Creek was dry when we hiked the trail in May, but the Forest Service claims that during a normal season the creek is flowing in May and dries later in the summer. There is a pipe leading to a horse trough that was half filled with muddy water.

Continue on, remaining fairly level then up a small incline to a saddle and Wilderness boundary (no sign) at 2.8 miles. Now the Snake River is visible. Head to the right, following the well-defined trail and dropping at a gradual to moderate rate. There are a lot of trails here so stick to the slopes heading down to the river. At 3.5 miles cross over another saddle and see the end of the trail and road below. Cross a fence shortly before reaching the trailhead at Dug Bar at 4.3 miles. A marker points out the trailhead.

(Those who would like to camp at Dug Bar will find a campsite with access to the Snake River and a pit toilet less than 0.5 mile down the road. Also, there's another site through the gate leading to Dug Bar Ranch, and on down past the ranch to the Snake River and end of the road. This is the historic site of the Nez Perce crossing in 1877.)

Lone Pine Saddle from Nee-me-Poo Trail

13 DUG BAR TRAILHEAD TO DEEP CREEK RANCH

Distance: 10.1 miles (one-way)
Elevation gain: 3,160 feet, loss 1,760 feet
High point: 3,360 feet
Usually open: All year, but snow can close some of the higher passes during the winter months.
Topographic map: Hells Canyon Wilderness Map
Obtain map from: Hells Canyon National Recreation Area or Wallowa-Whitman National Forest

This trail provides wonderful views of the surrounding Hells Canyon Wilderness, leads to scenic Deep Creek Ranch, across some flower-covered slopes (in spring), and there is little poison oak to travel through. All add up to a fine trail.

To reach the trailhead at Dug Bar, drive Wallowa Road east from Joseph, Oregon, for 30 miles to the small town of Imnaha. Here you'll find a cafe, gas, and a store. Turn left (north) on paved lower Imnaha Road and follow this to FS Road No. 4260 at 6.5 miles. Now the road to Dug Bar is somewhat rocky, narrow, and steep. It is also slippery when wet and 4-wheel drive is recommended for traveling in these conditions. Trailers are not recommended, but passenger cars can reach the trailhead if they negotiate the last 10 miles carefully and can climb steep grades.

After 1.6 miles enter Hells Canyon NRA and another 11.9 miles down the road cross a bridge, the Imnaha River now on the west side of the road. In 2.8 miles pass the Nee-Me-Poo National Historic Trailhead (see #12, Nee-Me-Poo Trail, for details), then continue another 7.8 miles to Dug Bar Trailhead, located just before the closed gate. Here you'll find room to park, access to the Snake River, a place to camp if you so desire, and a pit toilet.

The trailhead to Deep Creek is located next to the gate. A sign reading, "Lord Flat-13, Pittsburg-25, and Saddle Creek-47," points the way. Follow Snake River Trail No. 1726 along the fence towards Dug Bar Ranch, located at the end of the dirt road. Head around to the right of the ranch and through a gate at 0.4 mile. Follow the winding trail up the open slope to another fence at 1.0 mile. This is also the Wilderness boundary.

Begin a gradual climb around a series of slopes then descend before reaching Fench Gulch at 2.0 miles. Gradually climb from there then descend across a large open flat area. While you are hiking look for elk, deer, and rattlesnakes.

Reach a junction to Lord Flat at 2.8 miles. Follow Western Rim National Recreation Trail No. 1774 (also known as Summit Trail) to 3.2 miles and Dug Creek. (This is also the junction to Deep Creek Ranch.) Dug Creek is a good place to camp with water nearby although the creek wasn't flowing much in May. There is quite a bit of poison oak in the area, but it can be avoided quite easily.

Cross the creek and head up the steep slope to the east, now hiking Deep Creek Bench Trail No. 1707. Reach a flat area and a dry camp at 3.8 miles. Gradually climb to 3.9 miles then wind around a number of slopes, staying level or gradually climbing again. Reach Robinson Gulch at 4.7 miles. Now it's a steep climb up a series of switchbacks, then the trail leads moderately to a fence and saddle at 5.6 miles.

There are a variety of wildflowers during the climb and elk are often visible, too. Head down to Coyote Gulch and water (usually flowing through the summer except in dry years) at 5.9 miles. Gradually head up and down or remain level to 6.9 miles then begin a moderate, occasionally steep descent to Little Deep Creek at 7.7 miles.

This is a good site for a camp. There is plenty of water, flat areas for a tent, and a few big ponderosa pines for shade.

To continue to Deep Creek Ranch, cross Little Deep Creek and head up the moderate to steep slope then level off at 8.3 miles. Hike another 0.5 mile for a view into Deep Creek drainage and the ranch. Descend the moderate slope to Deep Creek Ranch at 10.1 miles.

There is a camp site here, but the Forest Service claims it gets trashed out every so often. A spring is located north of the old ranch house; however, the water has not been tested by the Forest Service.

Deep Creek Ranch

14 FREEZEOUT TRAILHEAD TO BEAR MOUNTAIN

Distance: 8.4 miles (one-way)
Elevation gain: 3,495 feet; loss 200 feet
High point: 6,895 feet
Usually open: June through October
Topographic map: Hells Canyon Wilderness Map
Obtain map from: Hells Canyon National Recreation Area or Wallowa-Whitman National Forest

A hike, or better yet backpack trip, to Bear Mountain provides each visitor with one thing that many of us backpack for—a terrific view. Although portions of the trail pass through the trees, most of the hike is in the open where the surrounding scenic terrain can be viewed as you climb up to Bear Mountain.

To reach Freezeout Trailhead (open all year), drive from the intersection of Oregon Hwy. 82 and Wallowa Road in Joseph. Go east on Wallowa Road for 30 miles to the tiny town of Imnaha and your last chance for supplies. Here you will find a cafe, store, and gas pumps.

Turn right on Upper Imnaha Road (County Road No. 727), a gravel road which leads south to FS Road No. 4230 in 12.7 miles. Turn left on Road No. 4230, driving this good dirt road to the trailhead at 3.0 miles.

A new trailhead was being built when we hiked the trail in May of 1988, with completion projected for later during the summer. There will be plenty of room to park, a pit toilet, and a new sign pointing the way to both trails in the area. (Please note, the winter of 1987/1988 was exceptionally dry, permitting us to hike this trail earlier than in a normal year.)

Begin Saddle Creek Trail No. 1776, a moderate to steep grade up the open slope to the junction of Western Rim Trail No. 1774 at 2.2 miles. Just before the junction you'll come to a fork in the trail. The trail leading to the right meets up with Western Rim National Recreation Trail (also known as the Summit Trail) about 0.1 mile south.

Back at the junction, notice the terrific view before heading right (south) on Western Rim Trail No. 1774. To the east, see Bear Mountain. And next to Bear Mountain (on the left) the summit of Black Mountain. Saddle Creek drainage is located to the northeast and Hat Point is located to the north. Also, there's a wonderful view looking back toward the trailhead.

Now the trail remains level or climbs gradually across a mostly forested slope and meets with another trail at 3.3 miles. Keep to the left, hiking at a moderate rate across the open slope. At 3.8 miles there is a good view looking back toward the Imnaha Valley.

The trail finally levels off at the summit and reaches the junction to Trail No. 1763 at 5.0 miles. Stay on Trail No. 1774, heading level or slightly downhill to Bear Mountain Trail junction at 5.9 miles.

There are a couple of good camps near the junction, both located in the trees near a creek that normally flows all year, but may dry up later in the summer during a dry season. Both camps are used by elk hunters in the fall. Horse owners will find a cattle trough at the head of the creek.

Notice all the burnt trees here and at nearby Squirrel Prairie. Named for all the squirrels that inhabit the area after the snow melts, the area was burned in a 1973 fire which charred over 20,000 acres. Called the "Freezeout Burn," the fire burned from this location, down the Saddle Creek drainage, and up over to Hat Point.

To continue to Bear Mountain, hike Bear Mountain Trail No. 1743, crossing the creek and climbing the moderate slope to the ridgetop. The trail follows along the top or to one side of the ridge, passing through scattered burnt trees, as well as stands of pine. The trail remains level or climbs gradually to 6,895 feet and the summit of Bear Mountain at 8.4 miles. From here the view is terrific. See the Snake River drainage below, the Seven Devils Mountains of Idaho, and over to Hat Point.

(Those that desire may want to climb the summit of nearby Black Mountain. At 6,862 feet, the summit lies 0.8 mile away and can be reached by descending 495 feet then climbing 462 feet.)

Bear Mountain and Black Mountain from Freezeout Saddle

15 FREEZEOUT TRAILHEAD TO HAT POINT (VIA THE WESTERN RIM TRAIL)

Distance: 9.6 miles (one-way)
Elevation gain: 3,622 feet; loss 240 feet
High point: 6,982 feet
Usually open: June or July through October
Topographic map: Hells Canyon Wilderness Map
Obtain map from: Hells Canyon National Recreation Area or Wallowa-Whitman National Forest

Although Hat Point can be reached by a steep dirt road during the summer months, we decided to hike from Freezeout Trailhead via the Western Rim National Recreation Trail (also known as the Summit Trail). Western Rim Trail is a typical trail for some of the hike and is combined with FS Road No. 4240 for portions of the hike as well. As a result, some of the trail is located in the Wilderness, and some of it, including Hat Point, is located just outside the Wilderness in Hells Canyon National Recreation Area.

Although heavy snows block the trail and road to Hat Point until June or July in an average year, we were able to hike into the area in late May. However, the road was covered with at least two feet of snow in places, and in one instance we had to hike over snow for nearly two miles. Struggling through knee-deep snow, we reached Hat Point before anyone could drive there and found our efforts well rewarded. We had a terrific view all to ourselves!

To reach the Freezeout Trailhead (open all year), drive from the intersection of Oregon Hwy. 82 and Wallowa Road in Joseph, Oregon. Drive east on Wallowa Road for 30 miles to the tiny town of Imnaha and your last chance for supplies. Here you will find a cafe, store, and gas pumps.

Turn right on Upper Imnaha Road (County Road No. 727), a good gravel road which leads south to FS Road No. 4230 in 12.7 miles. Turn left onto No. 4230, driving this good dirt road to the trailhead at 3.0 miles.

A new trailhead was being built when we hiked the trail in May of 1988. Scheduled for completion during the summer of 1988, there will be plenty of room to park, a pit toilet, and a new sign pointing the way to both trails in the area. (Please note, the winter of 1987/1988 was exceptionally dry, permitting us to hike this trail earlier than in a normal year.)

Begin hiking Saddle Creek Trail No. 1776, a moderate to steep grade up the open slope to the junction of Western Rim Trail No. 1774 at 2.2 miles. Just before the junction you'll come to a fork in the trail. Head left and up the saddle to the Wilderness boundary sign, trail sign, and junction.

Notice Bear and Black Mountains to the east, the Saddle Creek drainage to the northeast and Hat Point located to the north. Also, there's a wonderful view looking back toward the trailhead.

From the junction head left, climbing the moderate grade across an open slope, then traveling across a semi-open slope at 2.7 miles. Cross over to the opposite side of the ridge at 3.2 miles, climbing a moderate grade through the trees. As you hike look to the west, watching for the small, distant towns of Joseph and Enterprise.

Reach the junction of FS Road No. 4240, which now serves as the Western Rim Trail, at 4.2 miles. Also, note that the remainder of this trail is not located in the Wilderness.

It's a gradual climb to Saddle Creek Campground at 4.6 miles, a small campground with a big view. Also, there are picnic tables, fire rings, and pit toilets. From here it's a gradual up and down to Memaloose NRA Helitack Base at 7.9 miles. Continue another 0.1 mile to the junction of Hat Point.

Turn right on FS Road No. 315 and follow this to FS Road No. 332 at 9.5 miles. Reach the Lookout Tower and campground at 9.6 miles. This scenic campground does not have running water, but there are picnic tables, fire rings, and a pit toilet located near the parking area. Also, there is water at Sacajawea Spring 0.3 mile north of Hat Point via the Rim Trail.

Visitors are allowed to climb the tower for an even better view of the surrounding area. Atop the tower, built in 1948, you are now an additional 90 feet above the summit, the highest point in Oregon from which the Snake River is visible. From the top of Hat Point, at 6,982 feet, it's a drop of over one vertical mile to the Snake River below. Also, see the Seven Devils Mountain of Idaho, and the Wallowa Mountains of Oregon to the west.

Western Rim Trail

16 WESTERN RIM/ HAT POINT/ HIGH TRAIL LOOP

Distance: 24.9 miles (complete loop)
Elevation gain: 5,742 feet; loss 5,922 feet
High point: 6,982 feet
Usually open: June or July through October
Topographic map: Hells Canyon Wilderness Map
Obtain map from: Hells Canyon National Recreation Area or Wallowa-Whitman National Forest

This loop trail is outstanding in many ways. From the beginning of the hike, at Freezeout Trailhead, there are superb views, and from Hat Point get a peek into the deepest gorge in North America, a drop of over one vertical mile. Along High Trail hike over semi-open benchlands, across open slopes, and over a few scenic streams.

To reach Hat Point from Freezeout Trailhead please see #17 FREEZEOUT TRAILHEAD TO HAT POINT. These instructions will take you to Hat Point at 9.6 miles.

From the signed junction in the campground at Hat Point, begin a long, but gradual descent down Hat Point Trail No. 1752. Switchbacks make the trail a pleasant one to descend. Notice signs of the old trail to see how steep the trail once was before it was rerouted in 1974.

Enter the Wilderness at 9.9 miles. While descending the forested slope, look for occasional views into the Snake River drainage far below. At 11.8 miles be sure to head off the trail 100 feet or so, climbing a rock outcrop for a fantastic view of the Seven Devil Mountains and the Snake River. From this point the switchbacks lead down at a gradual to moderate rate to a fork of Hat Creek at 12.2 miles. Switchback over or near the creek several more times before reaching the junction of Hat Point Trail and High Trail at 13.3 miles.

There's plenty of room to camp near this junction and water from a nearby fork of Hat Creek. Also there is an old sheep cabin here, called "The Trough" by the local Forest Service. Heading down from Hat Point, the sign is difficult to see and could easily be missed.

Turn right on High Trail No. 1751 (sign reads No. 418) and hike past the cabin then gradually up and down or level to Hat Creek at 13.9 miles. This creek, as well as the others mentioned along this loop, usually flow all year. However, they could run dry by late summer after an especially dry winter.

High Trail is pleasant for hiking with a mostly level grade and some gradual ups and down. On occasion there is a moderate climb also. The trail passes through scattered stands of ponderosa pine, a sprinkling of wildflowers during late spring/early summer, and there are spectacular views as well.

At 14.9 miles cross Rough Creek then climb moderately to a flat, grassy area at 15.5 miles. Now the trail heads to the right, hugging the slope. This trail is much more difficult to see than the one that stays straight, reaching a flat camp in the trees. If you reach the camp, turn around and head back about 150 yards. Once you find the trail it's very definite for the remainder of the hike. From this point you can see Freezeout Saddle to the southwest.

Continue across the open slope, crossing small streams at 16.0 and 16.1 miles. Continue to Twobuck Creek at 17.0 miles. There's a semi-flat area where a person could camp on the bluff overlooking the creek, but there is a better camp at Log Creek, a short distance ahead.

Head up the steep slope now to the second fork of Twobuck Creek at 17.1 miles. The trail flattens out after this section and continues to Log Creek at 18.0 miles. Although we found some trash in the area, this is one of the only flat areas for camping with water nearby. Also, there is an established fire ring.

To continue, hike the open terrain at a grade typical of the past few miles, reaching another creek at 18.3 miles, Big Creek at 19.5 miles, and another creek at 20.3 miles. In each drainage there are trees for shade, a welcome relief when the sun is shining down relentlessly.

Reach the junction to Saddle Creek at 20.9 miles. Notice all the trees burned in the "Freezeout Burn," of 1973. Over 20,000 acres were burned in this fire. Today, there are American kestrels living in the snags, as well as pink-chested Lewis woodpeckers, and many other species.

From the junction of Saddle Creek Trail No. 1776, the trail begins at a gradual grade, becoming moderate later on with an occasional steep section. Although most of the area is open, there are a few trees for shade. Reach Freezeout Saddle at 22.7 miles. To complete the loop, descend to Freezeout Trailhead at 24.9 miles.

Hiker at Hat Point overlooking Snake River

17 FREEZEOUT TRAILHEAD TO THE SNAKE RIVER (VIA SADDLE CREEK)

Distance: 9.5 miles (one-way)
Elevation gain: 1,760 feet; loss 3,720 feet
High point: 5,360 feet
Usually open: May through November, although the lower portions of the trail and trailhead could be open at least 10 months of the year. If you are willing to hike through deep snow on Freezeout Saddle you could hike the trail before May.
Topographic map: Hells Canyon Wilderness Map
Obtain map from: Hells Canyon National Recreation Area or Wallowa-Whitman National Forest

Scenic vistas, the sweet sound of the rushing waters of Saddle Creek, and the awesome Snake River can all be enjoyed during this hike. Every hiker should be alert for rattlesnakes, and those allergic to poison oak should watch for the plant along the lower Saddle Creek drainage and along the Snake River.

To reach Freezeout Trailhead (open all year), drive from the intersection of Oregon Hwy. 82 and Wallowa Road in Joseph, Oregon. Drive east on Wallowa Road for 30 miles to the tiny town of Imnaha and your last chance for supplies. Here you will find a cafe, store, and gas pumps.

Turn right on Upper Imnaha Road (County Road No. 727), a good gravel road which leads south to FS Road No. 4230 in 12.7 miles. Turn left on Road No. 4230, driving this good dirt road to the trailhead at 3.0 miles.

A new trailhead was being built when we hiked the trail in May of 1988, with completion projected for later during the summer. Now there will be plenty of room to park, a pit toilet, and a new sign pointing the way to both trails in the area. (Please note, the winter of 1987/1988 was exceptionally dry, permitting us to hike this trail earlier than in a normal year.)

Begin hiking up Saddle Creek Trail No. 1776, a moderate to steep grade up the open slope to the junction of Western Rim National Recreation Trail No. 1774 (also known as Summit Trail) at 2.2 miles. Just before the junction you'll come to a fork in the trail. Keep left and you'll be at the junction in no time.

From the saddle (also the Wilderness boundary), notice the terrific view before heading down the east side of the saddle. Hat Point is seen to the north, Bear and Black Mountains to the east, and destination Saddle Creek drainage to the northeast.

To continue to the Snake River, remain on Saddle Creek Trail, descending the moderate and sometimes steep slope to the High Trail junction at 4.0 miles. Head straight toward the bluff then down the south side following the trail as it gradually switchbacks down near Saddle Creek. Although the trail is never far from Saddle Creek, access to water isn't always easy for there is either a steep slope leading to water or an abundance of downed trees, brush, etc.

The trail passes through an area that was burned in 1973 in a fire named the "Freezeout Burn." At this time over 20,000 acres were charred. At 4.8 miles the trail forks, the left trail leading to a camp, Saddle Creek Trail heading to the right and gradually descending to Big Creek at 5.3 miles. Now the trail passes by an occasional ponderosa pine, but is mostly in the open.

The trail heads straight toward the Snake River, but occasionally a switchback leads down through a steeper portion of drainage, keeping the trail at a constant gradual grade. At 5.4 miles reach a camp on the right near a ponderosa pine and reach another camp at 5.6 miles, again on the right.

At 6.1 miles the trail leads down near the creek again and enters dense vegetation. But the thick shade doesn't last for long. Soon the trail leads across either an open or semi-open drainage.

At 6.4 miles cross Log Creek then reach another camp at 6.6 miles. Ford Saddle Creek at 6.9 miles and again at 7.3 miles, now hiking back on the north side of the creek. Again there's a camp near a ponderosa on the left, this one at 8.0 miles. Someone built a fire ring directly under the tree. Please don't use it!

Reach a junction to Battle Creek and the upper portion of the Snake River at 8.7 miles, crossing Rough Creek about 200 feet farther east. Hike straight ahead to complete this trail.

At 9.1 miles there are a few flat areas for camping with Saddle Creek nearby. However, watch for poison oak which lines much of the creek, creating a nasty barrier. Continue on to 9.5 miles and a bluff overlooking the Snake River. This is a wonderful spot for camping. There are plenty of flat sites with a lovely view and creek water close by.

Saddle Creek drainage from Freezeout Saddle

18 SADDLE CREEK/SLUICE CREEK/HAT POINT LOOP

Distance: 31.8 miles (complete loop)
Elevation gain: 7,822 feet; loss 7,822 feet
High point: 6,982 feet
Usually open: June through October
Topographic map: Hells Canyon Wilderness Map
Obtain map from: Hells Canyon National Recreation Area or Wallowa-Whitman National Forest

This loop provides many things, most of all variety. There are terrific views from Freezeout Saddle and Hat Point, and the chance to gaze at the steep canyon walls that keep the mighty Snake River on track. Sit along the Snake for a while, watching the rapids that thrill adventure-seeking rafters each year. Those with the desire to reach high places in a single day may want to hike from the dry reaches of the Snake River canyon, to Hat Point, an elevation gain of 5,542 feet.

The trail begins at Freezeout Trailhead then heads 9.5 miles via Saddle Creek to a bluff overlooking the Snake River. Follow #17, FREEZEOUT TRAILHEAD TO THE SNAKE RIVER (via Saddle Creek Trail), for the first portion of the loop.

From the junction of Saddle Creek/Snake River Trails, head north on Snake River Trail No. 1726. Reach the junction of Trail No. 1752 at 9.9 miles. This trail leads to Hat Point.

Stay straight, following the trail as it hugs the canyon wall above the Snake, where shade is at a minimum and temperatures extreme during the summer months. The trail is mainly a gradual up and down with an occasional moderate incline. Cement steps help one climb up and down in the moderate sections, although some hikers have complained that the steps are too high. The Forest Service set these cement steps in place, hauling them up from the Snake River, in 1973. Their purpose is to hold down rock, providing safer footing for hikers and horseback riders, alike.

Notice McGaffee Cabin across the river at 10.5 miles then reach Marks Creek at 11.3 miles. Marks Creek was dry in May of 1988 when we hiked the trail, but the Forest Service reports that the creek normally runs dry in July.

Reach another junction to Hat Point, via Trail No. 1753 at 12.4 miles. Also, at this point see Waterspout Rapids. At 14.5 miles come to Sluice Creek junction. There are plenty of campsites available in this area with water available at Sluice Creek. (If camping in the area, or resting before heading up to Hat Point, you may want to hike another 0.5 mile down the trail to Rush Creek rapids and a view of Johnson Bar. This area can be viewed, later on, from Hat Point.)

To reach Hat Point, head up Sluice Creek Trail No. 1748 and into dense vegetation before reaching Sluice Creek cabin at 14.7 miles. Also, you'll find poison oak in this drainage until you reach higher ground in the next couple of miles.

Continue up at a gradual rate then head away from the creek and up the open slope at a moderate to steep grade at 15.2 miles. Although there is an occasional switchback, most of the trail just angles up the slope. At 15.8 miles reach an area where the trail is difficult to find due to thick grass. Head up to two ponderosa pines to catch the well-defined trail at this point.

The trail continues up at a moderate to steep grade, entering the trees at 16.2 miles. A nice change from the dry slopes traveled over previously, the forest offers shade and the chance to stop and scan the nearby slopes for elk which seem to be everywhere.

At 17.9 miles head out into the open again, traveling a gradual to moderate slope and reaching the junction to High Trail No. 1751 at 18.3 miles. Keep straight, hiking High Trail at a gradual grade through the trees to the junction of Hat Point at 18.5 miles. There are plenty of scenic camps here with a wonderful view and creek water at a fork of Hat Creek.

To continue to Hat Point and another good camp, stay right at the sign and head right again 100 feet or so up the trail. The well-defined trail leading past the cabin is High Trail No. 1751. (While Hat Point is the destination on this loop, it is possible to remain on High Trail, hiking this scenic trail back to the junction of Saddle Creek, up to Freezeout Saddle and back to the trailhead. From this point it is a 11.6 mile trip back to the trailhead. See #16, WESTERN RIM/HAT POINT/IIIGH TRAIL for specifics on High Trail.)

Head up Hat Creek Trail No. 1752 at a gradual grade through the trees, two high points of this trail. The shade is welcome and so is the easy hike, especially if you are hiking from the Snake River. At 19.6 miles cross a small stream and continue up to a rock outcrop, located just off the trail, for a grand view at 20.0 miles. Continue up to 21.9 miles and the Wilderness boundary. Now the trail heads out of the Wilderness and up to Hat Point at 22.2 miles.

At Hat Point the view is out-of-this-world as you peer over one mile down into the Snake River drainage. Also, visible are the Seven Devils Mountains of Idaho, the Wallowa Mountains of Oregon, and much more. There's a 90-foot tower to climb if you so desire and camping facilities, too. These include picnic tables, fire rings, and a pit toilet. Water is not available at Hat Point unless you hike the trail when snow covers the ground like we did. Those hiking after the snow melts will have to walk 0.3 mile to Sacajawea Campground, located north of Hat Point via the Western Rim Trail, to get water from a spring.

To continue on the loop, hike FS Road No. 332 to FS Road No. 315 at 22.3 miles. Turn left, descending gradually or remaining level and reaching the junction of FS Road No. 4240 at 23.8 miles. (The Forest Service roads you've been traveling now serve as the Western Rim National Recreation Trail, also called the Summit Trail.)

Turn left, reaching Memaloose NRA Helitack Base at 23.9 miles. Hike on past the base, following the road as it descends gradually, remains level, or occasionally climbs gradually up and down. Along the way, there are some views into Hells Canyon.

Reach Saddle Creek Campground, a nice facility with a grand view, picnic tables, fire rings, and a pit toilet at 27.2 miles. Continue past the campground, reaching the junction for Western Rim National Recreation Trail No. 1774 at 27.6 miles. Turn left off the road, now hiking a standard trail at a moderate grade, across a semi-open slope. Look for the towns of Joseph and Enterprise to the west.

At 28.6 miles reach a saddle, descending the south slope now, and reaching Freezeout Saddle at 29.6 miles. Turn right, heading back to the trailhead at 31.8 miles.

Young buck mule deer

INTRODUCTION TO THE MILL CREEK WILDERNESS

Steep ridges and canyons, along with many small streams and lovely meadows form much of Mill Creek Wilderness, with a nearly flat plateau (Bingham Prairie) located in the northwest corner. In addition, one can visit the unique rock outcrops known as Twin Pillars and Whistler Point. And best of all, crowds are few.

Located 20 miles northeast of Prineville, Oregon, Mill Creek Wilderness was designated as such on June 26, 1984 when President Reagan signed the Oregon Wilderness Act of 1984. Prior to wilderness status the area was classified as a Special Management Area.

Twenty miles of trails lead visitors throughout this 17,400 acre Wilderness, managed solely by the Ochoco National Forest. Trails include Twin Pillars Trail, a National Recreation Trail since 1979, Belknap Trail, and Wildcat Trail. The Forest Service maintains the trails on a yearly basis.

The Wilderness is located within the southwestern extension of the Blue Mountain Range and is composed of roughly 85 percent mixed conifer forest. The remaining portion is mostly open barren ridge tops. Much of the timber consists of old-growth forest of Douglas-fir and ponderosa pine, with lodgepole pines dominating the northwest corner plateau. While hiking in this area you will undoubtedly notice a lot of dead or dying trees. This is due to an infestation of mountain pine beetles.

The elevation ranges from a low of 3,725 feet along East Fork Mill Creek to a high of 6,240 feet near the view point in the northeast corner of the Wilderness. East Fork Mill Creek, a tributary of Ochoco Creek, flows through the center of the preserve, and begins life near the northern portion of the area, then flows southwest through Wildcat Campground.

The best time for hiking Mill Creek is usually from May through October. While higher elevations may experience some lingering snow later in the spring, most of the preserve is usually snowfree by May or June. In the summer, look for highs to be from 75 to 85 degrees with lows in the 40's. Winter temperatures are cold with high and lows ranging from 50 degrees above zero to 15 degrees below zero.

Those interested in snow sports such as cross-country skiing or showshoeing will find that Mill Creek Road (FS Road No. 33) is plowed during the winter months, leading to access at Wildcat Campground. A four-wheel drive vehicle is necessary, though, to get to FS Road No. 27 just north of the Wilderness.

Spring, summer, and fall visitors will find an abundance of activities to enjoy. There's the chance to do some fishing, look for pretty wildflowers, day hike, backpack, pan for gold, look for rocks, ride horses, and in the fall, hunt for various game.

There are 22 miles of streams in the area. Small rainbow and brook trout are found in all of the perennial streams with the Forest Service rating the fishing as "poor to good." Habitat is below potential in certain areas due to shading and instream woody debris.

Due to the varied terrain, including an abundance of riparian areas, there is a variety of animal life, most of it typical of the Blue Mountain Range. Bird species include pileated woodpeckers and goshawks, American robins, tanagers, and more. Wild turkeys were introduced a couple of years ago and are reportedly "doing fair."

Mammals include the rarely seen black bear and mountain lion. Also there are badgers, porcupines, marmots, and the area provides spring, summer, and fall range for deer and elk.

Those who don't care to hike with domestic cattle should be forewarned that the area receives moderate cattle use from August to October.

And those seeking solitude will want to visit anytime except during the fall hunting season when the area becomes quite crowded with hunters, all seeking that special trophy.

There are several small surface gemstone claims in the Wilderness. Primitive roads lead to four general areas in which the claims are located. These include Whistler Spring-Desolation Canyon, White Rock, Twin Pillars, and Forked Horn Butte. Thundereggs, Oregon's state rock, and agates, are the primary gems mined.

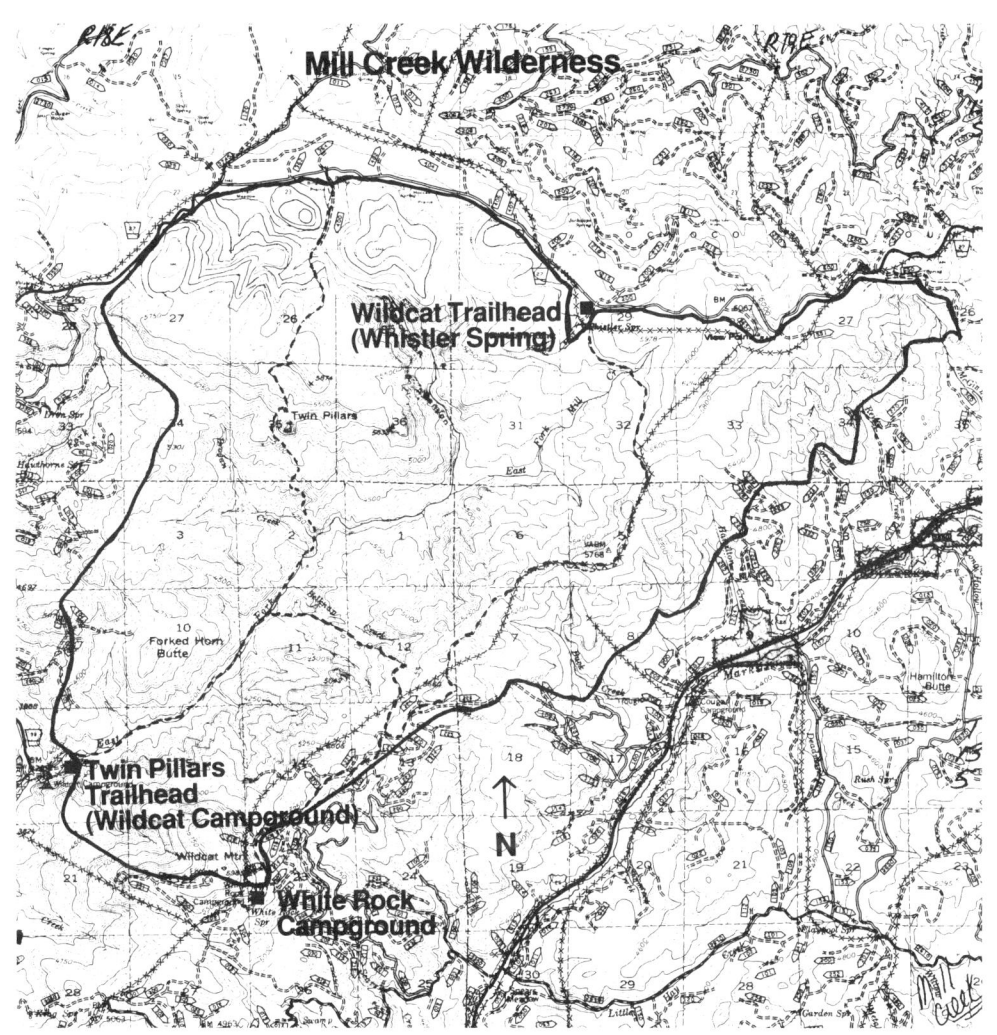

For more information contact the following:

Prineville Ranger District
Ochoco National Forest
2321 E. Third
Prineville, OR 97754

or

Forest Supervisor
Ochoco National Forest
P.O. Box 490
Prineville, OR 97754

19 TWIN PILLARS NATIONAL RECREATION TRAIL

Distance: 8.5 miles (one-way)
Elevation gain: 2,100 feet; loss 347 feet
High point: 5,800 feet
Usually open: May through October
Topographic map: U.S.G.S. Opal Mountain, OR - 1968 (and) U.S.G.S. Ochoco Reservoir, OR - 1948
Obtain maps from: U.S.G.S. — Denver, Colorado

On this trail you will go through old-growth forest carpeted with grass, hike along the East Fork Mill Creek for several miles, walk beside lush meadows, and view spectacular Twin Pillars, a unique volcanic plug.

To reach the trailhead at Wildcat Campground, head east from the junction of U.S. Hwy. 26 and U.S. Hwy. 126 in Prineville, Oregon. Drive Hwy. 26 through town, where you'll find gas, food, and other supplies readily available, and reach Mill Creek Road at 10.2 miles. Head north to Wildcat Campground, driving the paved road to 5.2 miles. Continue straight traveling the gravel road (FS Road No. 33) another 5.6 miles to the Wildcat Campground turnoff. (Before reaching the turnoff notice another unique volcanic plug, Steins Pillar, to your right.)

There is a large area for trailhead parking a hundred feet or so from the main road. Wildcat Campground is located just ahead with flat campsites, picnic tables, fire rings, and pit toilets available for a small fee.

Begin hiking Twin Pillars Trail No. 832 at the sign. The trail skirts along the edge of East Fork Mill Creek, crosses over the road, then heads back into the trees. Reach a gate and the Wilderness boundary at 0.2 mile. If you open the gate, please close it. Hikers will find steps leading over the fence.

Ford East Fork Mill Creek at 0.3 mile then cross a spring at 0.9 mile. At 1.0 mile ford East Fork Mill Creek again.

Twin Pillars Trail leads through dense old-growth forest at times. At other times you'll pass under large stands of ponderosa pine, thick growth of lodgepole pine, and throughout much of the trip lush grasses blanket the forest floor and wildflowers (in May and June) brighten the trail. The majority of the streams, springs, and creeks encountered on this route flow year-round.

The trail leads gradually up or level to numerous bridge crossings over East Fork Mill Creek at 1.2, 1.3, 1.4, 1.5, and 1.8 miles. Then again there is a bridge over another creek at 2.8 miles. Also, you'll find the junction to Belknap Trail No. 832A. In addition, there is a camp near the junction.

At 3.1 miles cross the bridge over East Fork Mill Creek and at 3.2 miles begin a short, but steep climb. Hike a gradual to moderate grade up then level off for a view of Twin Pillars to the north at 3.8 miles.

Now descend to a stream at 3.9 miles and begin a moderate climb to another stream at 4.3 miles. Continue up, climbing a series of switchbacks. Level off somewhat at 5.0 miles for another view—through the trees—of Twin Pillars. At 5.3 miles reach a sign pointing to Twin Pillars. Scramble up the slope for a close-up view of the Pillars.

Continue up the slope at a moderate grade then gradually climb to 6.2 miles. Now the trail remains level or descends gradually until you reach the end of this trip.

At 7.0 miles reach an old road and shortly thereafter a meadow on the right. At 7.2 miles see Desolation Canyon to your right and farther on step near the edge if you so desire for a peek into the canyon itself.

Cross the old road again at 7.6 miles and two streams, one at 7.7 miles and one at 7.8 miles. Notice Bingham Prairie to your right as the trail winds around to the west side of the prairie, remaining in the trees. Reach FS Road No. 27 at 8.5 miles.

Upon reaching this point you can turn around and hike back to Wildcat Campground, with a shuttle to pick you up there, or you can hike back via Wildcat Trail, making one big loop around the Wilderness.

To complete a loop linking Twin Pillars and Wildcat Trails, turn right on Road No. 27, walking 0.2 mile to Bingham Springs turnoff. Just down FS Road No. 400 (about 0.1 mile) you'll find a good spot to camp with tasty spring water. To reach Wildcat Trail continue up Road No. 27 another 2.6 miles to FS Road No. 500 and the turnoff for Wildcat Trail and Whistler Spring. The trailhead is located 0.1 mile from the junction. The spring is located 0.3 mile down Road No. 500. See #20 WILDCAT TRAIL, and #21 BELKNAP TRAIL to complete loop.

Twin Pillars

20 WILDCAT TRAIL

Distance: 8.1 miles
Elevation gain: 900 feet; loss 1,350 feet
High point: 5,750 feet
Usually open: May through October
Topographic map: U.S.G.S. Lookout Mtn., OR - 1951 (and) U.S.G.S. Ochoco Reservoir, OR - 1948
Obtain map from: U.S.G.S. — Denver, Colorado

Although Wildcat Trail can be hiked from either the north or south end, we opted to hike north to south, making one large loop through the Wilderness. For information on traveling this loop see #19, TWIN PILLARS NATIONAL RECREATION TRAIL AND BELKNAP TRAIL.

Wildcat Trail leads from a point near Whistler Peak, a unique geological formation, through dense forest, across open ridges, and provides some nice views of the Wilderness and forest beyond. From several points along the trail it is possible to see the Cascade Range.

To reach the trailhead near Whistler Spring, drive 32 miles east on U.S. Hwy. 26, traveling from the junction of U.S. Hwy. 26 and U.S. Hwy. 126 in Prineville, Oregon. Supplies are available in town.

Turn left (north) on FS Road No. 27 and continue up to Wildcat Trailhead located about 6.5 miles from Hwy. 26 on FS Road No. 500. Turn left again and reach the trailhead in 0.1 mile. Whistler Spring is located another 0.2 mile down the road and flows year-round.

Begin hiking at the trail sign, descending at a gradual rate through the trees, across a meadow, and back in to the trees. At 0.7 mile there is a view into the East Fork Mill Creek drainage with Whistler Peak barely visible to the west and Wildcat Mountain easily seen to the southwest. Also, Steins Pillar is visible to the right of Wildcat Mountain and on a clear day you can see the Cascades in the distance.

Gradually descend to East Fork Mill Creek at 0.9 mile. (This is the only reliable water source until the trail ends at White Rock Spring.) Continue on, gradually climbing to another point and a good view of Whistler Peak at 1.5 miles.

Now it's a gradual up and down to an open area and good view at 2.4 miles. Occasionally there are flowers along the trail, mostly lupine, and balsamroot, and a few irises as well.

Continue across the semi-open slope now, for a good view of Twin Pillars at 2.5 miles. From here the trail gradually descends then switchbacks down one time at 3.2 miles.

It's a gradual up and down to a gate at 4.8 miles. Cross, now entering a large stand of ponderosa pines then back into a forest of Douglas-fir and pine. At 6.0 miles reach Belknap Trail. There's a small sign on a tree pointing to the right and over the fence. Instead of trying to reach the trail from this point, continue 100 feet farther to another sign and a gate. Belknap Trail begins here. See #21, BELKNAP TRAIL for further information.

At 6.2 miles the trail is blocked because of a big earth slide that happened two or three years ago. A makeshift trail heads up and around the slide. A new trail will be installed in the future according to the Forest Service, but a definite date hasn't been set.

At 6.7 miles cross a small spring. Continue up to the Wilderness boundary at 7.4 miles, now hiking an old road. At 7.8 miles the road forks, head left, soon hiking a standard trail to White Rock Spring at 8.1 miles. The spring is located to your left as you enter White Rock Campground. There's piped water at the trough (usually flows year-round) and a picnic table, fire ring, pit toilet, and plenty of room to camp nearby.

21 BELKNAP TRAIL

Distance: 2.3 miles
Elevation gain: 0 feet; loss 1,250 feet
High point: 5,250 feet
Usually open: May through October
Topographic map: U.S.G.S. Lookout Mountain, OR - 1951
Obtain map from: U.S.G.S. — Denver, Colorado

Belknap Trail begins and ends in the middle of the Wilderness and is accessible from both Wildcat Trail and Twin Pillars Trail. We used the trail to complete a loop that extended from Wildcat Campground to Bingham Prairie, over to Whistler Spring, south to White Rock Campground, and then down Belknap Trail to Twin Pillars Trail and back to Wildcat Campground. See #19, TWIN PILLARS NATIONAL RECREATION TRAIL and #20, WILDCAT TRAIL for more information.

Belknap Trail No. 833A leads through old-growth forest with some openings for views into the Wilderness.

From Wildcat Trail No. 833 descend at a gradual to moderate grade, hiking through the trees. At 0.8 mile begin hiking across a semi-open slope. There's a nice view of Twin Pillars looking to the northwest at 1.1 miles. Throughout the next mile or so there will be more views of the Pillars.

Before reaching Twin Pillars Trail No. 832 at 2.3 miles, the trail steepens. At the junction of Twin Pillars Trail you'll find plenty of water at East Fork Mill Creek and a camp nearby.

Meadow off the Belknap Trail

INTRODUCTION TO THE MONUMENT ROCK WILDERNESS

Golden eagles soar on high, American kestrels flutter their streamline wings then pounce on mice, and coyotes howl. Elk and deer roam the land, robins flit about, and evening grosbeaks visit campsites. These species, along with grouse, hawks, badgers, bear, and the rare wolverine live in the Monument Rock Wilderness.

Monument Rock Wilderness is located in eastern Oregon, about 30 miles east of John Day. Managed by the Malheur and Wallowa-Whitman National Forests, the area consists of 19,650 acres. Established with the passage of the 1984 Oregon Wilderness Act, 12,620 acres are located in the Malheur National Forest, 7,030 acres in the Wallowa-Whitman National Forest.

Ranging in elevation from 5,120 feet on the Little Malheur River to 7,873 feet atop Bullrun Rock, the area is comprised of ponderosa pine forests in the lower elevations and subalpine species along the higher ridges and peaks. The diverse habitat provides a haven for many animals and plant life as well. Because most of the animals found in the forest are shy and rarely seen, hikers shouldn't expect to view an abundance of wildlife. Of course, it's always nice just knowing that they are there.

From the higher points hikers will view other areas of the Wilderness, along with Strawberry Mountain Wilderness to the west. Unfortunately, much of the area surrounding the Wilderness has been logged, creating a less-than-pristine view at times.

There are three prominent rock points in the area. Table Rock, located just outside the Wilderness boundary, has a fire lookout on top which stretches to 7,815 feet above sea level. Currently, the lookout is staffed from June to November. Other prominent points include the highest peak, Bullrun Rock at 7,873 feet, and Monument Rock, at 7,736 feet, the peak for which the area was named.

Monument Rock Wilderness encompasses the headwaters of the Little Malheur River and the upper drainages of the South Fork of Burnt River as well. Rainbow trout inhabit the Little Malheur River where angling is considered fair to good. Migrating up the river from Beulah Reservoir to spawn, the larger trout swim downstream as the flow diminishes in the summer months.

While hiking the trails, especially along the river drainages, look for dwarf huckleberries. Also, crimson columbine, lupine, and many other species of wildflower and plant life.

A major eyesore in the Monument Rock area is the abundance of cattle grazing in the area. Some of the springs have been fenced to prohibit the bovines from actually stepping in the water, but still they are around, polluting the water, denuding the vegetation, and leaving huge cow piles on the trail. The problem is especially noticeable while hiking the outer sections of the Little Malheur River. If you'd rather not camp with bovines or dodge cow pies all day, the Forest Service recommends visiting the Wilderness during the early part of June before the cattle are released in the area.

There are relatively few trails, with the two best ones mentioned in this guidebook. Three other trails are located in the Wallowa-Whitman portion of the Wilderness but they are pack trails and very steep. The Forest Service recommends these be used for what they were originally intended—pack animals.

For more information contact the following:

Malheur National Forest
Prairie City Ranger District
Prairie City, OR 97869
(503) 820-3311

or

Wallowa-Whitman National Forest
Supervisor's Office
1550 Dewey Ave.
Baker, OR 97814

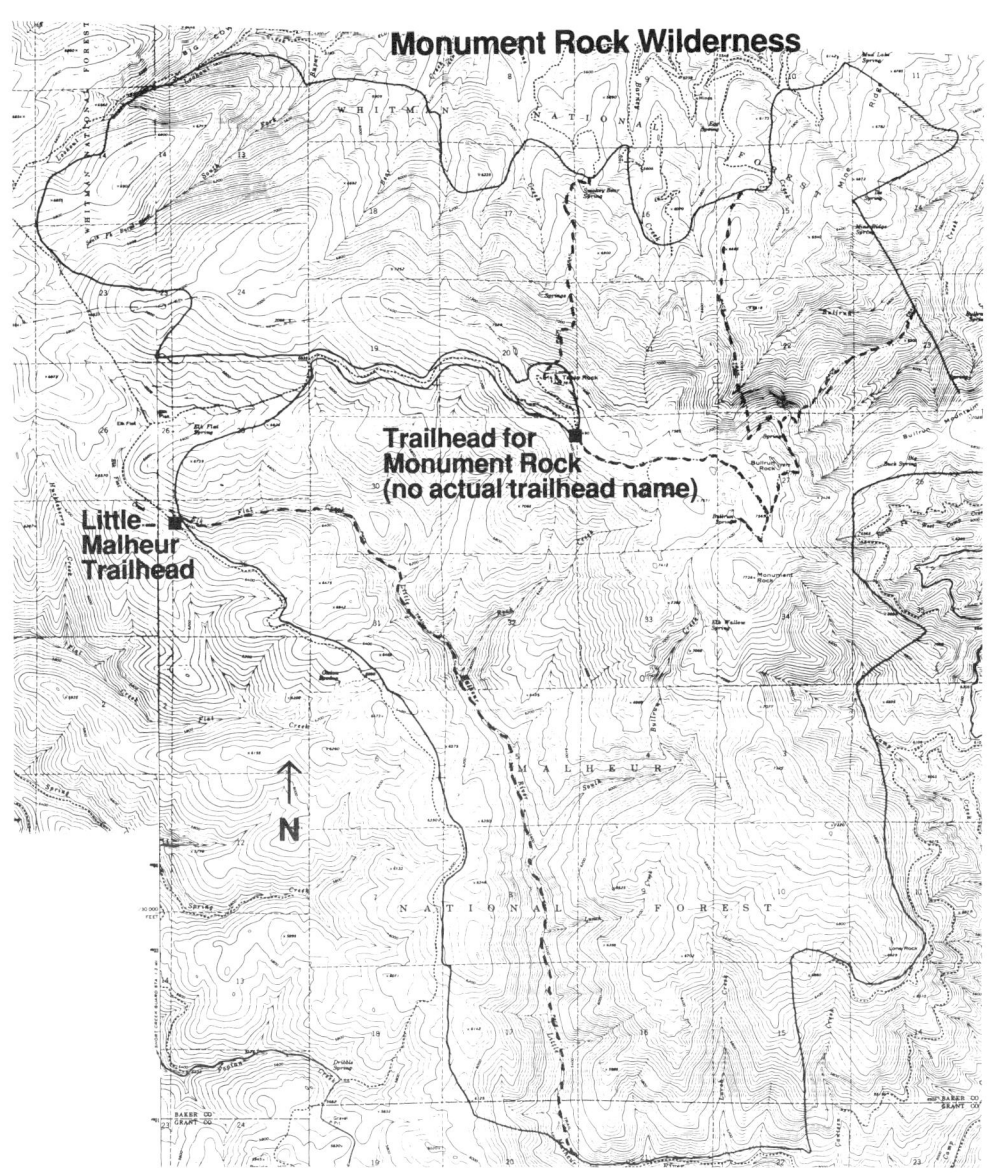

Little Malheur River

22 MONUMENT ROCK TRAIL

Distance: 2.2 miles (one-way)
Elevation gain: 75 feet; loss 165 feet
High point: 7,565 feet
Usually open: June through November
Topographic map: U.S.G.S. Bullrun Rock, OR - 1972
Obtain map from: U.S.G.S. — Denver, Colorado

There are some views of the Monument Rock Wilderness from this trail, but you'll have to share the trail with the cows that graze in the area. The Forest Service recommends: "Visit the area in early June when the water is flowing well and before the cows are turned out." Also, there's a better chance of viewing wildflowers.

To reach the trailhead for Monument Rock drive to Unity, Oregon, located about midway between Ontario and John Day on U.S. Hwy. 26. Reach the junction of U.S. Hwy. 26 and FS Road No. 6005 in the center of this small town of 105 people. (Gas and supplies are available.) Head west on paved FS Road No. 6005, driving 3.8 miles to a fork. Stay left on Road No. 6005 which is now well-maintained gravel. Proceed a couple of miles farther and enter the forest.

After 3.0 miles on the gravel road reach the South Fork Campground and another half mile or so up the road pass the Stevens Creek Campground. Keep to the left, staying on FS Road No. 6005, passing Elk Creek Campground also on the left. Sign "Rough Rd.—not recommended for vehicles—6 miles" is posted. (Although the road is rough, those with passenger vehicles may find it possible if they drive with care.)

Stay to the left as you pass two more forks before reaching FS Road No. 2652, 9.4 miles from the "rough road" sign. Turn left, reaching Elk Flat in another 2.0 miles. (Please note: Camping is not allowed at the trailhead but there are several sites here at Elk Flat.) Proceed left on FS Road No. 1370 for 3.6 miles to the trailhead. For a great view drive 0.7 mile past the trailhead, heading left up the road to the Lookout on Table Rock. At 7,815 feet, you can see for miles around from this point.

Back at the trailhead sign in at the registration box then hike down an old road which is in fact old Forest Road No. 1370 and is not officially designated as a trail. As you hike along you'll see the Strawberry Mountain range to the west and countless other peaks and valleys of northeast Oregon. Also, as you hike the first mile notice Monument Rock to the south, southeast.

Reach a trail junction at 0.6 mile. Trail No. 156 leads down an easy grade to Rock Creek Spring where you'll find room to camp. Rock Creek Spring was fenced in to keep the cows from destroying the spring, but the fence is partially down now. Fresh spring water enters a drum first which hopefully keeps the cows from getting into it.

Continue on Trail No. 1370 reaching another junction at 1.7 miles. Cross the barbed-wire fence, heading straight ahead and south to another junction at 1.9 miles. (The trail to the left isn't maintained and dead ends eventually, but someday the Forest Service plans to build a trail which will connect with the Little Malheur River Trail. See #23, Little Malheur River Trail for more details.)

Turn right at the junction reaching Bull Run Spring at 2.2 miles. There is room to camp near the spring which is also fenced to keep cattle out. From this point it's possible to bushwack about 0.5 mile south to the top of Monument Rock. Although very few people climb the 7,736 foot peak, it's a fairly easy hike.

23 LITTLE MALHEUR RIVER TRAIL (FROM NORTH TO SOUTH)

Distance: 7.2 miles (one-way)
Elevation gain: 200 feet; loss 1,300 feet
High point: 6,400 feet
Usually open: June through November
Topographic map: U.S.G.S. Bullrun Rock, OR - 1972
U.S.G.S. Little Baldy Mountain, OR - 1972
Obtain map from: U.S.G.S. — Denver, Colorado

Those hikers who love to explore small rivers may enjoy this trail, but should be aware of the damage done by cows grazing in the area. Meadows at both ends of the trail have been chewed down to nothing by the big bovines, but the middle portion of the trail is still lush and lovely. For the most enjoyable time visit the area in early June before the cows are turned out to pasture. Also, you'll have the best chance of viewing wildflowers then.

To reach the Little Malheur Trailhead drive to Unity, Oregon, located about midway between John Day and Ontario on U.S. Hwy. 26. You'll find the junction of U.S. Hwy. 26 and FS Road No. 6005 in the center of this tiny town of 105 people. (Gas and supplies are available.) Head west on paved FS Road No. 6005 for 3.8 miles to a fork in the road. Keep left, staying on Road No. 6005 which is now well-maintained gravel, entering the forest a couple of miles down the road.

Proceed another 3.0 miles to the South Fork Campground and another half mile or so up the road pass the Stevens Creek Campground. Keep to the left, remaining on Rd. 6005, and passing Elk Creek Campground on the left. Sign "Rough Rd.—not recommended for vehicles—6 miles" posted at this point. (Although the road is rough, passenger vehicles may find it passable if they drive with care.)

Stay to the left at two more forks then reach FS Road No. 2652, 9.4 miles from the "rough road" sign. Turn left again, driving 2.0 miles to Elk Flat. Head right on FS Road No. 1370, reaching the Little Malheur Trailhead 0.7 mile down the road.

You'll find plenty of parking near the trailhead with room to camp and fire rings already established. Sign in at the registration box then head down Little Malheur Trail No. 366. The trail passes through the trees on a level grade, occasionally heading through open meadows and crossing Elk Creek from one side to the next. It's easy to cross Elk Creek as it is usually dry except early in the season when the snow melts. (After hiking this trail in July, 1987, the Forest Service informed me that the trail was reconstructed and doesn't continually cross Elk Creek.)

At 2.0 miles the trail heads up a bluff then back into the trees. Climb the short rise then head down to the Little Malheur River at 2.1 miles. The trail continues to follow the river, crossing the river frequently. Usually the trail descends at an easy grade, sometimes remaining level, other times climbing for a short distance.

Campsites are limited during the first half of the trail due to the heavy vegetation and steep slopes. There's a good site between the trail and the river at 4.1 miles, but the best one is on a semi-open flat area at 4.7 miles. This is located just up the hill on the north side of the Bull Run Creek.

To continue on, cross Bull Run Creek and continue a mostly gradual downhill to the river which you'll cross at 5.2 and 5.5 miles. There's a lot of flat area from here to the trailhead, but some areas have been badly abused by cows. At 5.7 miles go through a gate (please close behind you).

Reach the Wilderness boundary at 7.1 miles, the trailhead at 7.2 miles. There is plenty of room to park at the trailhead, including room for horses, and room to camp.

INTRODUCTION TO THE NORTH FORK JOHN DAY WILDERNESS

The North Fork John Day Wilderness is a land of diversity. There are the high, craggy, granite peaks of the Greenhorn Mountains, the rugged gorge of the North Fork John Day River, and an abundance of wildlife. Known for its big game population of Rocky Mountain elk and mule deer, the area is also a superb fish habitat.

Three National Recreation Trails (Elkhorn Crest, North Fork John Day, and Winom Creek) meander through the Wilderness in which there are more than 130 miles of trail. (Hikers should note that mid-June marks the usual start of trail maintenance for the area which is generally completed by mid-September. The Forest Service recommends that people coming into the area, especially those on horseback, call ahead and find out which trails have been worked.)

The North Fork John Day Wilderness is located in the Blue Mountain Range of northeast Oregon and includes portions of the Elkhorn and Greenhorn Mountains. Supporting the largest and most important runs of anadromous fish in the John Day Basin, the North Fork John Day River winds through the geographic center of the 121,111 acre area.

Managed by both the Umatilla and Wallowa-Whitman National Forests, the Wilderness was originally designated as such on June 26, 1984 through enactment of Public Law 98-328, the Oregon Wilderness Act of 1984.

The North Fork John Day Wilderness is different from most others in that it is split up into four individual sections. Situated in the north, Tower Unit is the smallest of the four units with just over 8,000 acres. Few trails exist here and those that are available pass through dense stands of Douglas-fir, white fir, western larch, and lodgepole pine, providing little in the way of wide vistas. Because the trails in this section do not offer the quality trip found in other sections of the Wilderness (per the Forest Service) we concentrated our efforts in the other three areas. However, we did drive up to Tower Mountain, located just outside the Wilderness boundary and found the view from atop the 90-foot tower quite magnificent.

To reach Tower Mountain from Ukiah drive paved FS Road No. 53, 25 miles east to FS Road No. 5226 and the Tower Mountain cutoff. Follow this gravel road along the eastern edge of Tower Unit, reaching the top of Tower Mountain 8.0 miles up the road. The tower was built in the 1930's and is still in use today.

Directly south lies the Greenhorn Unit. Located in the Greenhorn Mountains, this unit consists of 13,911 acres, and also includes about 5,500 acres of the Vinegar Hill-Indian Rock Scenic Area. In this unit one can hike Saddle Ridge for wonderful views and look down upon Olive Lake, located just outside the Wilderness.

The lower slopes are heavily forested, the higher ridges open rocky areas with subalpine vegetation, subalpine fir, and whitebark pine. During the early summer months lush meadows provide hikers with the opportunity to see and touch delicate wildflowers. Also they can see the remains of the Fremont Powerhouse Pipeline.

Constructed in 1907 to generate electrical power to the thriving community of Granite and to the surrounding mines, the Fremont Powerhouse was the lifeline for the Red Boy Mines Company.

Although small in comparison with todays modern plants, the Fremont Powerhouse was the largest structure for miles around 81 years ago. About 83 feet by 28 feet, the structure was built for $100,000. with all materials and machinery transported from Baker by horse-drawn wagons.

Today, remains of the wood and steel pipeline that once transported water from Olive Lake to the powerhouse, eight miles away, can be seen along the road between the two points.

The Fremont Powerhouse last generated electrical power in October 1967 after 59 years of continuous service. The following year, the California Pacific Utilities Company donated the entire complex to the USDA Forest Service. Nominated to the National Register of Historic Places, the Powerhouse is currently maintained as a historic site, and is open to the public.

The largest unit, the North Fork John Day, is located between the Tower and Greenhorn units. Well over 85,000 acres strong, this portion is bisected by some 25 miles of the North

Fork John Day River Canyon. Over half of the acreage consists of gentle sloping tablelands and benchlands, the remainder is comprised mostly of steep ridges and side slopes melting into the river canyon.

The North Fork John Day supports a huge population of fish with an estimated 4,500 chinook and 10,500 steelhead migrating to the North Fork John Day River spawning grounds. The system provides good spawning and nurturing habitat for brook trout, rainbow trout, Dolly Varden, and whitefish.

Hikers may find old mining relics along the North Fork John Day River for this drainage was once a bustling gold and silver mining area in the middle to late 1800's. Thousands of folks removed an estimated $10 million in gold and silver.

Present day miners still work along the river; in fact, about 2,000 mining claims were on file at the time of designation in 1984. Several of these claims are considered valid and these folks are currently mining their claims.

Over 13,000 acres in size, Baldy Creek, the fourth and final unit is located due east of the North Fork John Day Unit in the Elkhorn Mountains. From Baker and Sumpter Valleys, the Elkhorn Mountain Range soars upward, its granite peaks stretching for the sky, reaching as high as 9,105 feet atop Rock Creek Butte.

This unit contains two vegetation divisions. On the lower slopes there are forest uplands dominated by Douglas-fir, western larch, white fir, lodgepole pine, and Engelmann spruce. Along the ridgetops of the east boundary of the unit, one will find subalpine forest dominated by whitebark pine, subalpine fir, and lodgepole pine. Also, there are stunted trees, low shrubs, and rock slides.

There are many bonuses to a visit in the North Fork John Day Wilderness, one of which is a lack of crowds. On a mid-summer day you're bound to hike for miles without seeing another soul. But in the fall, solitude is hard to find as the area is heavily-used by hunters.

Regardless of the season in which one visits there is always the possibility of observing wildlife. There are elk and mule deer, whitetailed deer, black bear, mountain lion, and occasionally there is a sighting of a mountain goat. A small herd of 16 mountain goats were introduced into the Elkhorns during the past five years, with two separate releases distributing the goats at Pine Creek. They were transported in from both Alaska and Olympic National Park.

Other species believed to be present include the Swainson's hawk and the American bald eagle. Although the bald eagle does not live in the Wilderness year-round, it does migrate through the area in the spring and early summer.

Like the animals that live here, hikers often find it necessary to cross streams and rivers. Sometimes a bridge is available, sometimes not. Hikers using this guidebook should note that some of the bridges mentioned in the following text may be torn down in the next few years. The Forest Service is working on a policy whereby some bridges may be completely removed, and others may have the rails removed, all to provide a greater wilderness experience.

Another change in this guidebook took place after our many trips into the Wilderness. Lightning struck throughout Oregon during the summer of 1987, causing thousands of fires, many of which touched Oregon's Wilderness areas. Marsha Kearney, District Ranger for the Umatilla National Forest in Ukiah, reports the following: "The recent fire has burned about 14,500 acres of the North Fork John Day Wilderness. Most of the burning has been a low intensity fire."

For more information contact:

Umatilla National Forest
2517 S.W. Hailey Avenue
Pendleton, OR 97801

or

Wallowa-Whitman National Forest
1550 Dewey Ave.
Baker, OR 97814

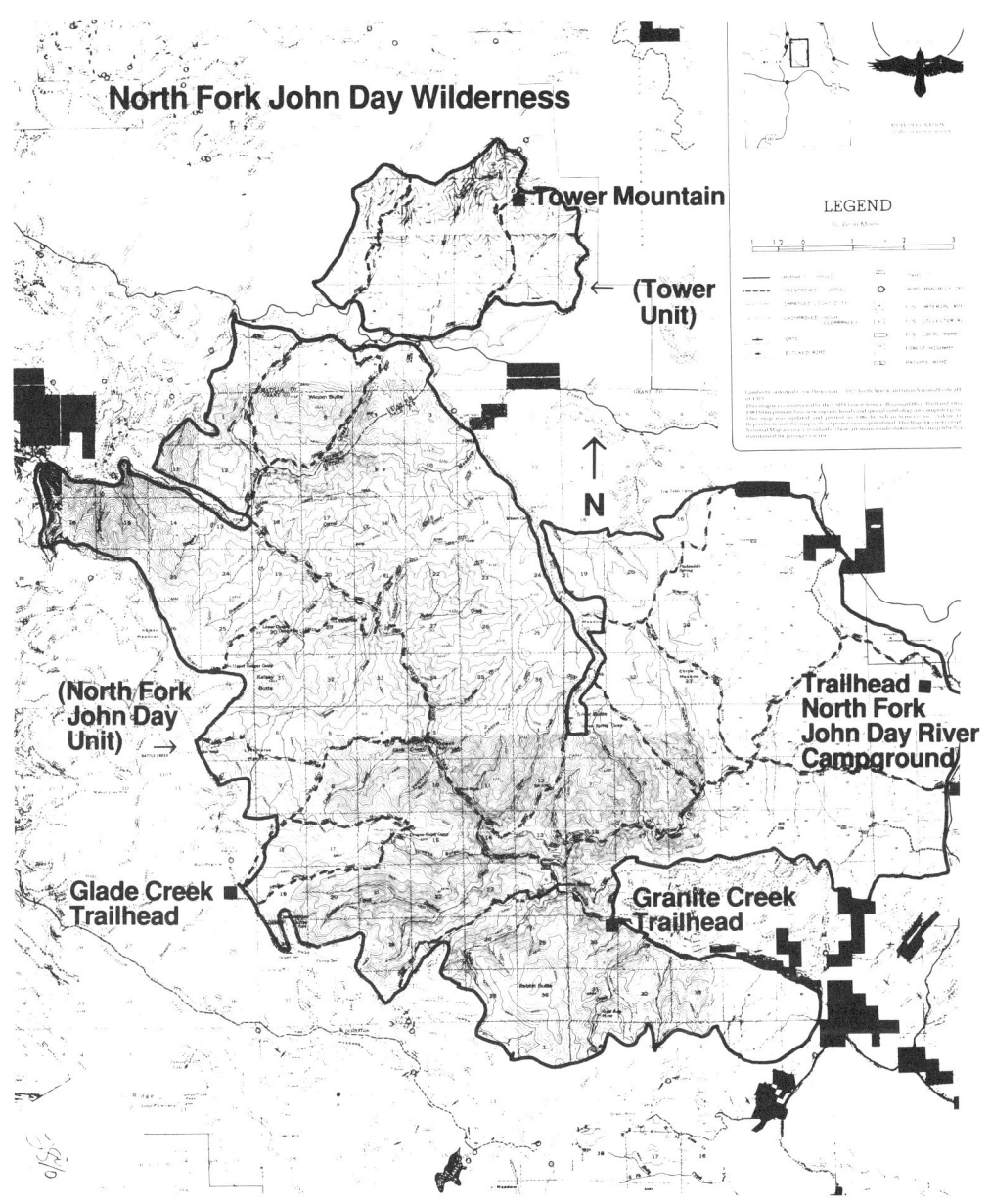

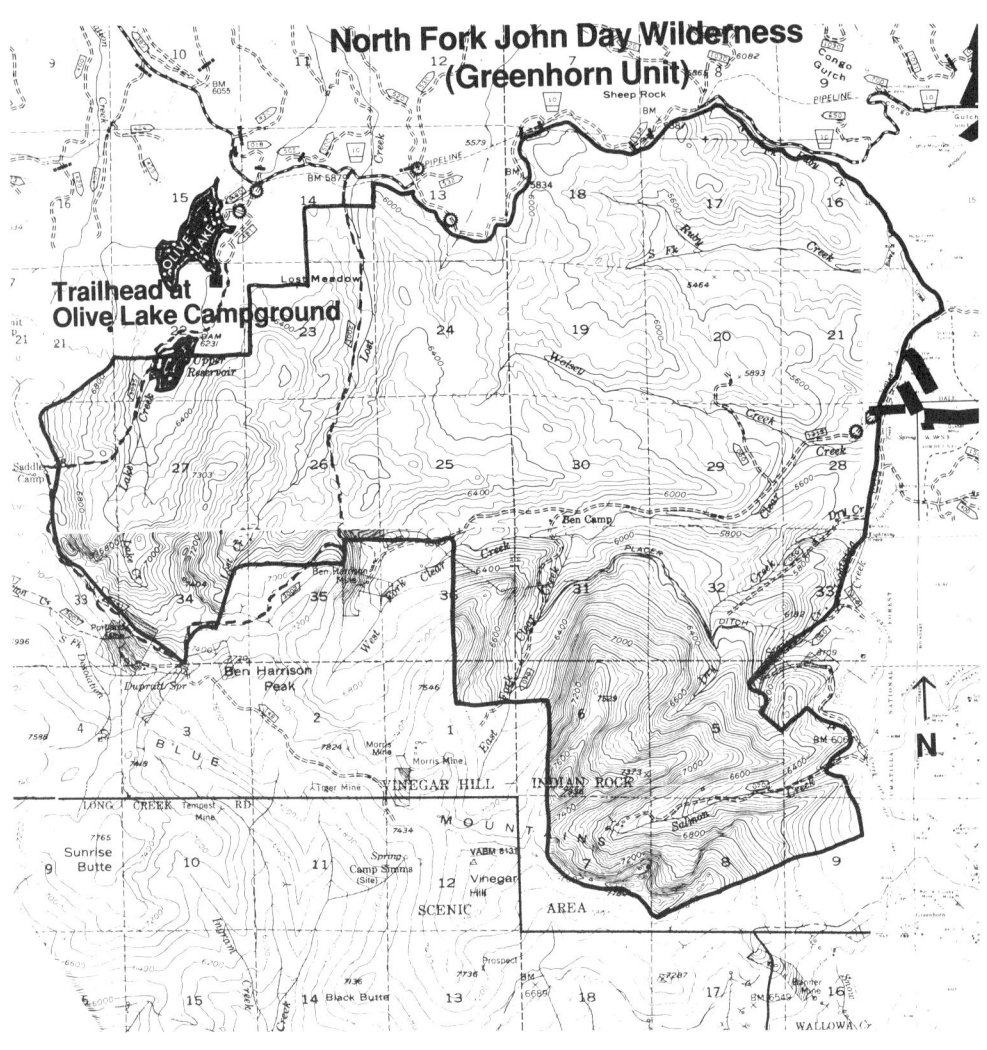

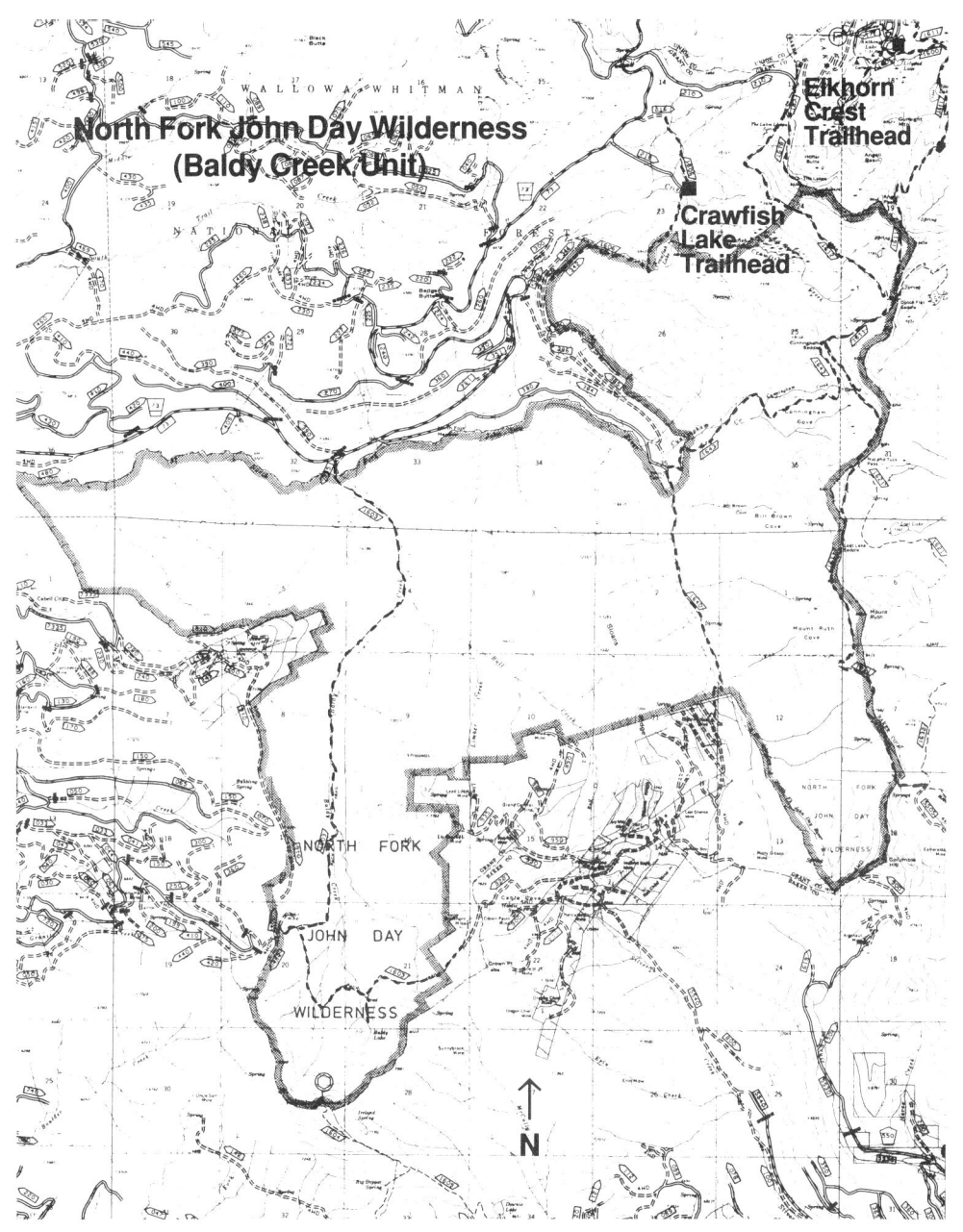

24 GLADE CREEK/ COLD SPRING LOOP

Distance: 9.1 miles (complete loop)
Elevation gain: 1,360 feet; loss 1,360 feet
High point: 6,560 feet
Usually open: Mid-June through November
Topographic map: North Fork John Day Wilderness Map
Obtain map from: Umatilla National Forest

This trip won't provide breathtaking scenes or wide vistas, but you will pass through dense stands of skinny lodgepole pines, and you might see Rocky Mountain elk and/or colorful wildflowers.

To reach Glade Creek Trailhead drive FS Road No. 10, a well-maintained gravel road, east from Dale, Oregon (gas and supplies available), for 11.6 miles. At this point the road forks. Turn left on FS Road No. 1010 and drive 8.0 miles farther to the trailhead. There is room to park here and a horse corral, too. Also, there is a horse trough with water from Cold Springs flowing into it.

Glade Creek Trail No. 3014 begins off the old road near the corral. Take the level to easy downhill trail through the trees and meadow where you'll find a variety of flowers. The trail is a bit difficult to find in some sections, but should be no problem for those who follow the rock cairns and blazed trees.

At 1.1 miles reach a small drainage. Piles of logged trees litter the area, located just outside the Wilderness boundary, so you'll want to head back into the trees as quickly as possible and continue the easy descent to 1.5 miles. To the left you'll see an area which was burned in the late 1970's. At this point it looks as though the trail could go right or left, but stay straight.

At 1.8 miles cross a creek and moderately descend to the junction of Cold Springs Trail at 2.1 miles. Glade Creek Trail No. 3014 continues to the left and on to the North Fork John Day River.

Turn right onto Cold Springs Trail No. 3008, climbing the easy trail through dense stands of lodgepole pine then leveling off. Moderately descend at 2.9 miles then level off again, reaching a meadow at 3.1 miles. Continue on a short distance farther and down a short moderate hill to a creek. There's a campsite off the spur trail near the creek with plenty of flat ground for a tent. This is evidently a hunters' camp as there are cut logs used for stools, a makeshift table, and a fire ring.

Back on the trail cross two streams then head up a steep hill which levels off shortly thereafter. Now the trail is an easy up and down to 4.9 miles and a junction with an old road. Keep to the right, hiking the road which now serves as the trail.

Continue up the moderate to steep grade, reaching two more junctions, one at 7.4 miles, one at 7.7 miles. Level off shortly thereafter then begin a gradual to moderate descent to Cold Springs Trailhead at 9.0 miles. Head right on FS Road No. 1010 and reach the parking area at 9.1 miles.

25 OLIVE LAKE/ SADDLE RIDGE/ LOST CREEK LOOP

Distance: 12.2 miles (complete loop)
Elevation gain: 1,500 feet; loss 1,500 feet
High point: 7,400 feet
Usually open: Mid-June through November
Topographic Map: No. Fork John Day Wilderness Map
Obtain map from: Umatilla National Forest

Anglers will especially enjoy this trip because the fishing at Olive Lake, the beginning and ending points for this loop trail, is great. And everyone should enjoy the fantastic view atop Saddle Ridge, with the flower-filled meadows below.

From Dale, Oregon (gas and supplies available here) travel 27.0 miles east on FS Road No. 10, a well-maintained gravel road, to FS Road No. 480 where you'll see a sign to Olive Lake. Turn right and continue straight past the fork leading to the boat dock, reaching the trailhead at roads end in about 1.0 mile. The road loops here and you'll find the trailhead at the end of the loop.

Those wanting to fish or camp at Olive Lake will find a free campground available with pit toilets, picnic tables, and fire rings. Although the fishing varies, it is generally good, with brown, brook, and cutthroat trout worth mentioning. Also, there are kokanee (landlocked sockeye salmon).

Back at the trailhead, begin climbing Saddle Camp Trail No. 3035, an old road, through the trees at an easy to moderate grade, occasionally descending at a slight angle. Cross a creek at 0.7 mile. Just before crossing the creek, about a few hundred yards prior, there is a campsite located through the trees near the meadow.

At 0.9 mile reach Upper Olive Lake which is mostly a large meadow, although the lake was dammed at one time and used as part of the water system associated with the Fremont Power Plant. (See INTRODUCTION TO THE NORTH FORK JOHN DAY WILDERNESS for more information on the Power Plant.) Continue through the trees along the west side of the meadow reaching the end of the road and the Wilderness boundary and sign at 1.4 miles.

Climb the easy grade, crossing two creeks at 2.0 miles. Now the trail climbs a moderate to steep grade with some flat sections, the ground covered at times with lush undergrowth. Reach another creek at 2.7 miles. The trail forks shortly thereafter, but both trails end up at the same point. Continue the steep climb to Saddle Camp at 2.9 miles.

There is plenty of room to camp at Saddle Camp. This is also the junction of Blue Mountain Trail No. 6141 which heads both north and south. Turn left (south) to continue the loop. Head up the hill and out onto a rocky outcrop at 3.3 miles for a good view of Upper Olive Lake.

Next, the trail follows the up and down contour of the land, passing through the trees and out into the open. Farther along hike through a fire-ravaged area, caused by a series of lightning-caused fires in 1986.

At 4.6 miles there is another good view of both Olive Lakes and the surrounding area, including Boulder Butte to the west. During the early summer there is a variety of wildflowers. At 4.9 miles begin walking an old road again, staying level or descending slightly to the junction of Lost Creek Trail No. 3002 at 5.3 miles.

Follow Trail No. 3002 to the northwest, again on an old road. The trail descends a steep slope then it's a gradual to level descent while hiking the edge of a meadow to a creek at 5.9 miles. At 6.0 miles the trail (road) forks. Turn left and descend the easy to moderate to steep slope.

At 7.3 miles the trail makes a big U-turn near the Ben Harrison Mine. Descend a steep trail to a junction at 7.4 miles and a sign, "Lost Meadow-2 miles, Desolation Rd.-4 miles." Turn left and soon the road turns into a trail again.

The trail passes mainly through the trees with occasional jaunts through a meadow. At 7.7 miles enter a meadow, following the old stumps across the soggy area. Head back into the trees, descending a steep switchback at 8.4 miles. Reach Lost Creek at 8.6 miles.

Cross the creek and follow it on the west side. Reach another meadow at 8.8 miles. The trail goes along the west side of the meadow then back into the trees. Reach Lost Meadow at 9.4 miles. Follow a few posts through the meadow then back to the trail along the creek.

At 10.0 miles leave the Wilderness. Notice the wooden pipes along the east side of the trail between the trail and river. These pipes were once part of the Fremont Power Plant mentioned previously.

At 10.5 miles the trail reaches FS Road No. 10. Turn left and hike back to the turnoff to Olive Lake at 11.3 miles. Turn left and follow the road back to the trailhead at 12.2 miles.

Olive Lake

26 NORTH FORK JOHN DAY RIVER CG TO WIND ROCK

Distance: 16.3 miles
Elevation gain: 700 feet; loss 1,529 feet
High point: 5,209 feet
Usually open: Mid-June through November
Topographic map: North Fork John Day Wilderness
Obtain map from: Umatilla National Forest

There are views of the North Fork John Day River while hiking this trail, as well as the opportunity to visit Granite Creek if you so desire. The fishing is good at both the river and creek with the chance of hooking Dolly Varden, rainbow, and brook trout. The Forest Service claims that this area, "is also inhabited by a native run of Chinook salmon."

Besides all this, there are old mining cabins and other mining paraphernalia to investigate. Please note, though, there are active mining claims in the Wilderness. Some, but not all, of the cabins located along the trail are open to the public. If you do use a cabin or two please leave the cabins in the same or better condition than when you first arrived.

The trailhead begins near the junction of paved FS Roads No. 52 and 73, 8.5 miles north of Granite, Oregon (gas and supplies available) via FS Road No. 73. There's a campground with pit toilets, picnic tables, and fire rings just prior to the trailhead and plenty of parking at the trailhead.

North Fork Trail No. 3022 begins at the end of a dirt road and the Wilderness boundary begins 100 feet farther. Walk another 100 feet and cross the river via logs, now hiking the north side of the river. At one time there was a bridge here, but in keeping with wilderness tactics the bridge will not be replaced. Also, the Forest Service reports that the bridges currently listed in this guidebook will eventually have the rails taken off of them. When they deteriorate they will not be replaced except for those where a river crossing might be dangerous.

It's an easy hike along the river. The trail is mostly level or slightly downhill with occasional climbs over rugged cliff edges. At 1.1 miles notice the miners cabins to the left. Farther on, at 2.2 miles, reach another cabin owned by the Hafers' of Blue Heaven Mines. This friendly couple allow visitors, but ask that visitors keep their place clean and put things back as they were found.

Past the Hafer's Mine cross Trout Creek via a bridge at 2.5 miles. As you hike along you've probably wondered about all of the bottle jars on the trees prior to and after this point. Inside the jars are photocopies of valid mining claims of the individuals who own the mines.

At 3.2 miles cross another stream and a nice place to camp. Just prior to this point and for several miles ahead, you'll notice that the forest was burned. Caused by lightning in 1986, the fire was named the Crane Fire because the fire began in the Crane Creek area. There was no attempt to douse the fire. Instead, it was allowed to burn, today providing valuable information to botanists and others, in understanding the "good" that fires can do.

Pass a couple of springs before switchbacking up and across a semi-open slope at 4.9 miles then switchback down to the river again. Notice all of the mining activity in this area, all part of the Thornburg Placer Mine. At 6.7 miles reach the junction of Crane Creek Trail No. 3011. This junction is hard to see as the trail is in a burn area. The easiest way to find the junction is to first find a sign on the trail you're now hiking which points the way straight ahead to Granite Creek and back to the Campground. Look here for a trail heading down to the river.

Just before reaching the Wagner Gulch Trail No. 3031 at 6.8 miles notice that the forest is now green again. Cross the creek via a bridge and reach an old cabin. Head straight past the cabin, staying on Trail No. 3022. A sign nearby states that this is Trail No. 6041. Disregard the sign, as this is still No. 3022.

At 7.2 miles there's another cabin, only this one is across the river. At 7.5 miles there are a few good campsites located between the trail and river. At 8.0 miles cross the bridge at McCarty Gulch. Again, there's plenty of room to camp just prior to the creek, between the trail and the river.

Continue to a nearly dry creek and cross via a bridge then on to Miner Blackwell Cabin, built in the 1800's, and another creek at 8.5 miles. Hike to the top of a bluff at 8.9 miles then back down along the river. Camps are sparse in this steep canyon. Take advantage of a camp at 9.5 miles if you like, although it isn't too big.

Soon after the sign pointing out Whisker Peak to the south, reach a sign for Tub Spring (now defunct) and another cabin at 10.6 miles. You're welcome to stay at the cabin, but it is a mess. A better camp, though, is just a short way ahead.

Although the trail continues on from the cabin, head down the trail near the cabin, ford the river and continue on the other side, reaching a sign "Bear Gulch" at 10.8 miles. There's a camp down near the river from this sign with a flat area for a tent. If you miss the trail by the cabin you'll find that the trail you were originally on will continue to the river. You can ford the river, although it is deeper, walk through the brush, and end up near the "Bear Gulch" sign.

Continue along the trail then reach a spring at 11.9 miles. Farther along reach the river and a large camp at 12.7 miles. Hike up the hill to a sign pointing out "First Gulch."

Hike down the slope now, noticing the good campsites on the sand bar. To reach this area descend to near river level at 12.9 miles and then head up river where there are plenty of flat campsites. At 13.7 miles reach lovely Granite Creek. There are corrals here, with room for horses, and plenty of room for camping. (If you'd like to take a side trip up Granite Creek see #27 GRANITE CREEK TRAILHEAD TO THE NORTH FORK JOHN DAY RIVER.)

To continue to Wind Rock turn right and head across the North Fork John Day River via a bridge at 13.8 miles. The trail passes some beautiful scenery here with steep rock walls and swift-moving water. Also, the vegetation is lush and beautiful. It's a relatively level hike, with some slight ups and downs, to the junction of Silver Hill Trail No. 3033 at 15.9 miles. Silver Butte is four miles up the trail.

Stay straight, crossing Silver Creek before reaching Wind Rock at 16.3 miles. Wind Rock may be difficult to find as it isn't as visible as one might hope for. There's a small creek to cross just prior to this high point where one can view Wind Rock through the trees. Those wanting to spend the night should head down the trail another 100 yards or so, hiking the spur trail to the river. Ford the river and camp on the opposite side. Also, several campsites were passed 0.2 mile before reaching Wind Rock.

Mine along the North Fork John Day River

27 GRANITE CREEK TRAILHEAD TO NORTH FORK JOHN DAY RIVER

Distance: 3.4 miles
Elevation gain: 80 feet, loss 544 feet
High point: 4,480 feet
Usually open: Mid-June through November
Topographic map: North Fork John Day Wilderness
Obtain map from: Umatilla National Forest

The hike from Granite Creek to the North Fork John Day River is scenic in spots with mining evidence in some areas. The fishing is quite good, with Dolly Varden, rainbow, and brook trout inhabiting the area along with a native run of Chinook salmon.

To reach the Granite Creek Trailhead drive northwest on FS Road No. 10, a well-maintained gravel road, from the junction of FS Roads No. 73 and No. 10 near the small town of Granite. (There's a store with gas and supplies in town.) At 1.5 miles turn north onto FS Road No. 1035. Take this for 4.2 miles to a fork then turn left on FS Road No. 010 and reach the trailhead in 0.3 mile. Local miners have made a road past the trailhead to the Wilderness boundary, a road that passes by all of their mining trailers and equipment as well. The Forest Service recommends you park here and hike the trail to the boundary. It's much more scenic as you hike through a semi-open forest of old-growth ponderosa pine instead of through the mining community.

Park at the end of FS Road No. 010 then hike across the semi-open slope to the Wilderness boundary and Indian Creek at 1.5 miles. From here begin an easy uphill then head across and down the semi-open slope dotted with ponderosa pines and some flowers. As you pass through this area you'll see obvious signs of mining activity, as well as several cabins and trailers. Also, notice Granite Creek to the left.

Cross a bridge over Granite Creek at 2.1 miles. The trail now skirts along the creek through an area rich in vegetation. A talus slope provides a pretty backdrop to the crystal-clear waters of Granite Creek. Hike up and then down another slope above the creek, crossing a creek where it flows into Granite Creek at 2.6 miles.

Continue on to Snowshoe Spring at 2.8 miles where a pipe delivers ice-cold water. Hike up the trail to the junction of Lake Creek Trail No. 3018 at 3.0 miles. This trail leads to FS Road No. 1010. Now head downhill, back to Granite Creek where you'll cross a bridge at 3.3 miles. Continue on to horse corrals, lots of campsites, and the John Day River at 3.4 miles.

Granite Creek

28 ELKHORN CREST TRAIL (FROM ANTHONY LAKE TO THE SOUTH WILDERNESS BOUNDARY)

Distance: 8.7 miles (one-way)
Elevation gain: 1,269 feet; loss 600 feet
High point: 8,100 feet
Usually open: Mid-June or early July through November
Topographic map: U.S.G.S. Anthony Lakes, Or. - 1972
Obtain map from: U.S.G.S.—Denver, Colorado

The Elkhorn Crest Trail is a real treat for one can see (on a clear day) the Cascade Mountain Range, including Mt. Hood to the west. There are several beautiful lakes to gaze down upon from the trail as well, and if you visit toward the end of summer you may hear elk bugling.

To reach the Elkhorn Crest Trailhead drive from Haines, Oregon. (Haines is a small town with gas and other supplies on hand.) At the junction of paved roads U.S. Hwy. 30 and County Road No. 411, drive 15.0 miles on Road No. 411, following the signs to Anthony Lake. (This road turns to FS Road No. 73 when you enter the forest.) Continue to the Elkhorn Crest Trailhead, 24.0 miles from Haines.

Hikers will find a nice campground at Anthony Lake with flat sites for tents, clean outhouses, and BBQ pits. Also, there is a day-use area with picnic tables and BBQ's, a boat rental establishment, cabins for rent, as well as a snack shop where one can get an ice cold drink, candy, or other snacks.

The trailhead for Elkhorn Crest Trail No. 1611 is located just before reaching the campground turnoff. A sign points the way.

Climb the easy trail through the trees reaching a junction at 0.5 mile. (The trail to the right heads back to Anthony Lake.) Continue straight, remaining on Trail No. 1611, and passing another junction in a few yards. Turn right to reach Black Lake, left to continue on Elkhorn Crest Trail. At 1.0 mile the trail passes above the east shore of Black Lake then levels off at 1.5 miles.

At 1.9 miles begin climbing a series of switchbacks, hiking past stunted, twisted pines embedded in the granite slopes. Reach a crest and the Wilderness boundary at 2.9 miles. There's a good view from here. Notice Angell Peak, the rocky peak to the northwest. To the north, see the valley below and Van Patten Butte. Looking west/southwest you'll see the Wilderness and points beyond.

Head across the slope at an easy to moderate grade, reaching the junction of Dutch Flat Saddle at 3.5 miles. Walk on over to the edge for a good view of Dutch Flat Lake and the Baker Valley below. Dutch Flat Creek Trail No. 1607 leads to the lake in 1.0 mile. Crawfish Trail No. 1612 heads to the right through Crawfish Basin and ends at FS Road No. 210.

Continue across the slope via the Elkhorn Trail and reach Cunningham Saddle at 4.2 miles. Cunningham Cove Trail No. 1643 leads to Peavy Cabin - 3.0 miles distant. Keep straight, though, heading across the level slope to Nip and Tuck Pass at 5.4 miles. Reach the junction for Lost Lake Trail No. 1621 at 5.5 miles.

Head across the open slope then switchback up at an easy to moderate grade. Cross to the west side of the ridge at 6.1 miles, continuing to Lost Lake Saddle at 6.2 miles and a good view of Lost Lake to the east of the saddle. From this point you may see Mt. Hood and several other of the large Cascade Mountain peaks to the west. Also, the Wallowa Mountains appear to the east and Big Lookout country to the southeast.

Climb gradually to 7.5 miles and again a good view. The mountain to the south/southwest is Argonaut Mountain. Continue down across the slope (covered with flowers in the summer) to the Wilderness boundary at 8.6 miles and a junction at 8.7 miles.

Although this guide ends here those who would like to explore farther should note that to the right, Peavy Trail No. 1640 leads to Peavy Cabin. Straight ahead (south) there's an old 4X4 road which leads to Cracker Creek and the old townsite of Bourne. And to the left one can continue on the Elkhorn Crest Trail No. 1611, hooking in with the North Powder River Trail No. 1632 which branches off the Elkhorn Trail.

Elkhorn Crest from the Elkhorn Crest Trail

29 CRAWFISH LAKE TRAIL

Distance: 0.5 mile
Elevation gain: 380 feet; loss 0 feet
High point: 6,980 feet
Usually open: Mid-June through November
Topographic map: U.S.G.S. Crawfish Lake, Or. - 1972
Obtain map from: U.S.G.S.—Denver, Colorado

Crawfish is a scenic lake, especially when seen from the south end, where Gunsight Mountain and Hoffer Butte create a splendid backdrop. Great fishing is another reason hikers should visit Crawfish Lake.

To reach the Crawfish Lake Trailhead drive 10.5 miles on paved FS Road No. 73 from the junction of FS Roads No. 73 and No. 52. Turn right on FS Road No. 218 and drive the bumpy road 0.8 mile to the trailhead. Although not the smoothest ride, the trailhead is accessible by passenger car.

From the parking area begin hiking Crawfish Lake Trail No. 1606 by crossing a log bridge, and again crossing a stream one hundred yards or so ahead. Climb the steep grade through the trees then level off and reach Crawfish Lake at 0.5 mile.

There's a nice campsite here and a good picnic site on a nearby rock bluff to the left. The trail continues around the west side of the lake, eventually leading to FS Road No. 320. There are some campsites at the south end of the lake where you'll get a magnificent view of Hoffer Butte and Gunsight Mountain.

Boys and their llama at Crawfish Lake

INTRODUCTION TO THE NORTH FORK UMATILLA WILDERNESS

Visitors to the North Fork Umatilla Wilderness find a rugged land where extremely steep, timbered canyons divide tree-dotted plateaus blanketed by native bunchgrass. Those visitors who enjoy fishing will find sizeable runs of anadromous fish, and Dolly Varden trout to their liking. Also, hikers find a variety of trails to explore.

Located 30 miles east of Pendleton, Oregon, this small 20,144 acre Wilderness has 27 miles of maintained trails to suit the needs of nearly everyone. Those who enjoy grand views will want to hike Ninemile Ridge. And, hikers who'd rather stay below will find lush vegetation draped around the various creeks that skirt through the lower portions of the area.

The North Fork Umatilla Wilderness was designated as such by Congress on June 26, 1984 and receives protection under the Oregon Wilderness Act of 1984. Listed as wilderness for a variety of reasons, high quality water was one of the major forces behind such classification. The North Fork of the Umatilla River supports sizeable runs of anadromous fish and also provides irrigation water for downstream agriculture.

Other wilderness streams include: Buck Creek, Bear Creek, Coyote Creek, and Johnson Creek. All of the above streams contain native trout and several have spawning steelhead.

The Wilderness is also known for it's excellent big game habitat (deer and elk) and is a popular hunting area each fall as hoards of hunters descend upon the region. An excellent summer range where calving, rearing, and breeding occur, the area is critical deer winter range as well.

Other mammals found here include cougar and black bear.

Bird life includes blue and ruffed grouse which are common. Also, there are eagles, owls, woodpeckers (including pileated woodpeckers), and a variety of song birds.

Abundant animal life is a result of the five major community types found within the Wilderness. Look for bunchgrass on shallow steep slopes, mixed conifer species, Ponderosa pine and associated species, and Subalpine fir.

Wildflowers bloom in spring and early summer. Although there are no records of rare and endangered plants found here, there are several plants identified as sensitive for this region. Look for Sabin's lupine, mountain ladys-slipper, (both common in the area), as well as Kruckeberg's sword fern.

Hikers—especially those hoping to capture flowers on film—should note that summers are intense in this area with highs averaging in the 80's, but often soaring to more than 100 degrees. June through September are the hottest months, with nighttime temperatures cooling down on even the hottest of days. For flower photographs, get up early or stay out late, thus avoiding the harsh rays of the mid-day sun.

For more information contact the following:

Umatilla National Forest
Supervisor's Office
2517 S.W. Hailey
Pendleton, Oregon 97801
(503) 276-3811

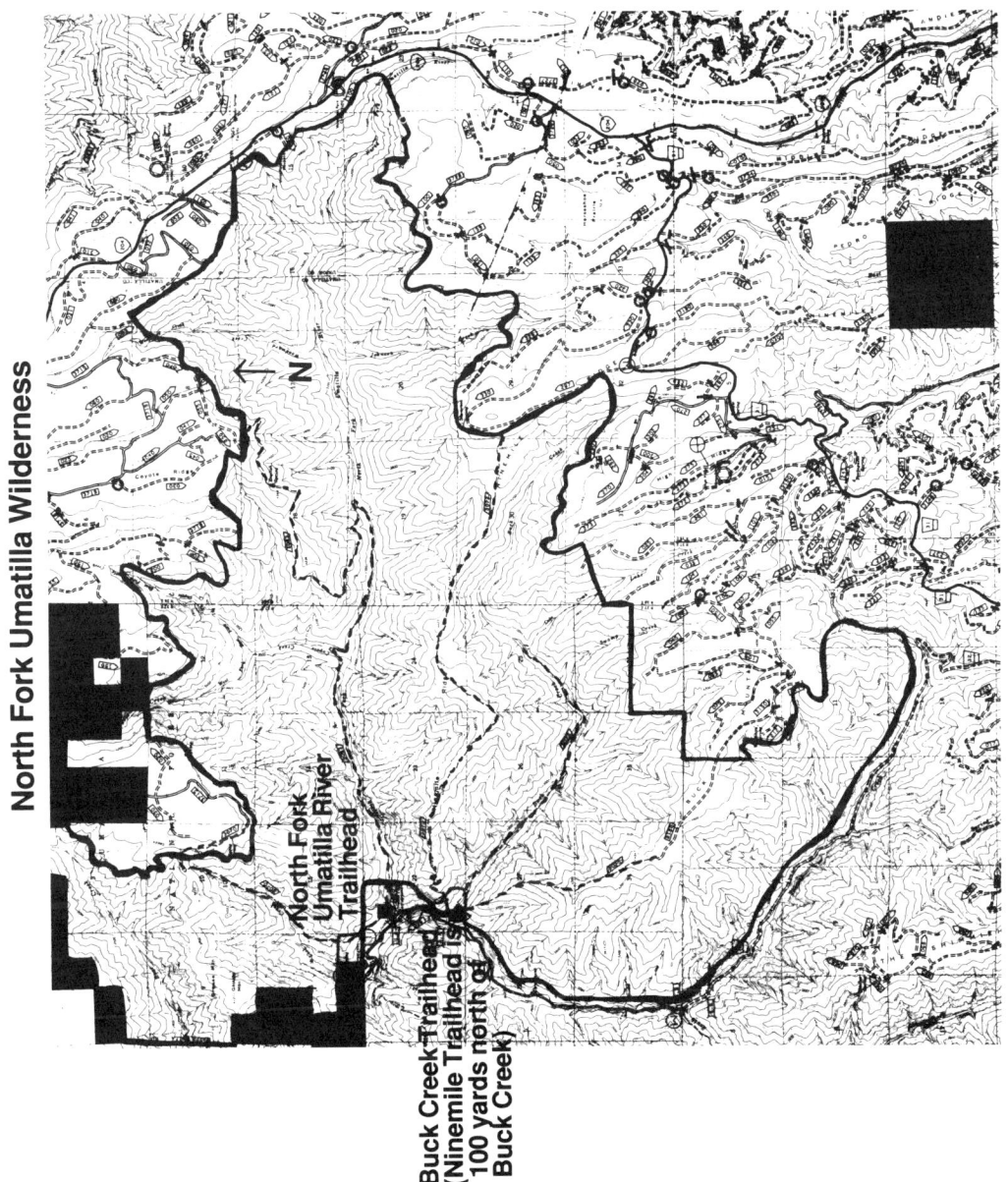

Hiker on Buck Creek Trail

30 BUCK CREEK TRAIL

Distance: 3.5 miles (one-way)
Elevation gain: 780 feet; loss 40 feet
High point: 3,180 feet
Usually open: June through November
Topographic map: U.S.G.S. Bingham Springs, OR - 1963
Obtain map from: U.S.G.S. — Denver, Colorado

There is an abundance of grouse, some deer, and also the chance to see pileated woodpeckers on this nice hike through dense vegetation. Also, tiny Buck Creek flows nearby and is seen often as there are numerous crossings over it.

From Oregon Hwy. 82 at Elgin, Oregon (where one can get supplies), head west on Oregon Hwy. 204. Drive 3.8 miles then turn left on FS Road No. 3738 (Phillips Creek Road). Take this good gravel road 10.5 miles to FS Road No. 31. Turn left onto paved Road No. 31 and drive to Ruckel Junction, another 3.8 miles. Turn right on FS Road No. 32, a bumpy road, but easily accessible with the average passenger car. After 6.8 miles it turns to good gravel. Arrive at the Umatilla Campground 3.4 miles.

At the campground you'll find nice campsites, piped water, picnic tables, BBQ's and fire pits. Upon reaching the south end of the campground turn right onto FS Road No. 415 and take this until it ends at 0.2 mile. Park at the trailhead near the Forest Service gate.

Begin hiking easy Buck Creek Trail No. 3073 which leads through the trees via an old road, then turns into a standard trail shortly thereafter. Reach the junction of Buck Mountain Trail in about 200 feet. Continue to the Wilderness boundary at 0.2 mile.

The trail is easy to follow as it skirts along Buck Creek, crossing it frequently from the north to south sides and back again. At 1.6 miles the trail leads up the middle of the creek then back onto dry land. Just before this point, there appears to be a trail on the right, leading away from the creek. Do not take this trail as it ends a short distance up the slope. Instead, continue straight up the creek.

Reach the end of the trail at 3.5 miles. The trail crosses the creek then slowly fades away. Lake Creek enters Buck Creek near the end of the trail.

EASTERN OREGON WILDERNESS AREAS

View north from Nine Mile Ridge

31 NINEMILE RIDGE TRAIL

Distance: 6.8 miles (one-way)
Elevation gain: 3,291 feet; loss 591 feet
High point: 5,100 feet
Usually open: June through November
Topographic map: U.S.G.S. Bingham Springs, Or. - 1963 and U.S.G.S. Andies Prairie, Or. - 1963
Obtain map from: U.S.G.S. — Denver, Colorado

Hikers with a passion for views will want to hike Ninemile Ridge. In addition to great views, one might also see grouse, deer, and other wildlife, plus wildflowers during the proper season. Be sure to carry water on this hike as there isn't any available on the ridge.

From Oregon Hwy. 82 at Elgin, Oregon (where one can get supplies), head west on Oregon Hwy. 204. At 3.8 miles turn left on FS Road No. 3738 (Phillips Creek Road). Take this good gravel road 10.5 miles to FS Road No. 31. Turn left on paved Road No. 31 and continue 3.8 miles to Ruckel Junction. Head right on FS Road No. 32, a bumpy but easily accessible road for the average passenger car. The road turns to good gravel after 6.8 miles and leads to the Umatilla Campground another 3.4 miles down the road.

At the campground you'll find piped water and plenty of campsites with picnic tables, BBQ's, fire pits, and pit toilets. Upon reaching the south end of the campground turn right on FS Road No. 415, driving until the road ends at 0.2 mile. Park at the trailhead near the Forest Service gate.

The trail leading to Ninemile Ridge is 100 yards or so back down FS Road No. 415. A sign does *not* point the way, however. Instead, dirt steps lead to the trail sign, located about 100 feet off the road. Ninemile Trail No. 3072 heads to the right, up the steep slope, and through the trees to the Wilderness boundary at 0.1 mile.

At 0.2 mile the trail becomes moderate with a few steep sections now and again. Wind around the semi-open slope, crossing several dry streams. At 2.1 miles the trail heads slightly down then up a steep slope. Level off and enjoy one of many wonderful views along this trail.

At 2.7 miles continue up a steep bluff, then switchback to a level spot at 3.5 miles. Now descend the easy slope, heading into the trees at 4.0 miles and arriving at an old hunter's camp at 4.1 miles. The trail fades out here, but is easy to pick up after crossing a grassy slope and continuing down into the trees at 4.2 miles.

Climb at 4.5 miles, then head across a slope and out into the open before leveling off at 4.7 miles. The trail forks at 5.0 miles. Head left at this point, beginning a series of slight ups and down.

At 5.6 miles begin a moderate up and down along a narrow semi-open ridge. Begin an easy climb at 6.0 miles then level off and head into the trees at 6.2 miles.

The trail climbs moderately through lush ferns at 6.4 miles then back out in the open again. Head up the easy to moderate slope to the top of the ridge and a trail sign at 6.8 miles. Exit the Wilderness about 100 yards back from this point.

32 NORTH FORK UMATILLA RIVER TRAIL

Distance: 4.0 miles (one-way)
Elevation gain: 510 feet; loss 50 feet
High point: 2.840 feet
Usually open: June through November
Topographic map: U.S.G.S. Bingham Springs, Or. - 1963 and U.S.G.S. Andies Prairie, Or. - 1963
Obtain map from: U.S.G.S. — Denver, Colorado

This hike allows for a scenic walk through dense vegetation with the pleasant sound of water bouncing off the rocky river bed. The wildlife is plentiful as well. Grouse and pileated woodpeckers enchant those who are lucky enough to see them and there are many other shy creatures inhabiting the area.

From Oregon Hwy. 82 at Elgin, Oregon (supplies are available here), head west on Oregon Hwy. 204. At 3.8 miles turn left on FS Road No. 3738 (Phillips Creek Road). Drive 10.5 miles on this good gravel road to FS Road No. 31. Turn left onto paved Road No. 31 and reach the Ruckel Junction in 3.8 miles. Stay right this time, driving FS Road No. 32, a bumpy road, but accessible with the average passenger car. After 6.8 miles the road turns to good gravel and makes the next 3.4 miles to the Umatilla Campground a breeze.

There is piped water and plenty of nice campsites at the campground. Also, there are picnic tables, BBQ's, fire pits, and pit toilets. Upon reaching the south end of the campground continue straight ahead 0.5 mile to the North Fork Umatilla River Trailhead.

Begin hiking through the trees via North Fork Umatilla River Trail No. 6143 and reach the Wilderness boundary at 0.2 mile. Continue, gradually heading up across an open slope for a short distance, then back into the trees for most of the remaining trip.

Reach a camp on the right near the river at 1.0 mile. Cross a creek at 1.2 miles and head left then right again. Note that there are more campsites in this area. At 1.7 miles cross another creek.

At 2.5 miles reach a large camp on the right. Continue 100 yards farther to Coyote Creek. Cross the creek, heading through old-growth forest and lush undergrowth. At 3.5 miles there is another camp on the right and an abundance of room to camp again at 4.0 miles.

Although the trail continues on from here it does not follow the river. Instead it heads up to Coyote Ridge. The trail passes through open slope and forested slope at a moderate grade with some steep pitches. Because the trailhead at Coyote Ridge Road is unimproved we recommend hiking the trail as listed in this guidebook.

Confluence of North Fork Umatilla River and Coyote Creek

INTRODUCTION TO THE STRAWBERRY MOUNTAIN WILDERNESS

Strawberry Mountain Wilderness is a magical place with much to offer. There are breathtaking views, crystal clear mountain lakes, red-tailed hawks soaring overhead, prairie falcons diving on unsuspecting prey, wildflowers, and the pleasant beauty of Canyon Creek.

Originally established in April, 1942, as the Strawberry Mountain Wild Area, the area first consisted of 33,000 acres. With the enactment of the 1964 wilderness act, however, the name was changed to the Strawberry Mountain Wilderness. In 1984, the Oregon Wilderness Act came into effect and the total acreage was increased to its present day size of 68,700 acres. Located east of John Day, Oregon, the Wilderness is managed solely by the Malheur National Forest.

From a low of 4,800 feet to a high of 9,038 feet atop Strawberry Mountain, the area is comprised of five of the seven major life zones found in North America, one of the few places in the Pacific Northwest where this occurs in such a small area. A visit to Strawberry will include everything from sagebrush and juniper, to ponderosa pine, lodgepole pine, and subalpine fir. In addition, there are countless species of plant life to observe, including an array of colorful wildflowers.

Strawberry Mountain dominates the area, holding honors as not only the highest point in the Wilderness, but the highest point in the Strawberry Mountain Range as well. A trip to the top of this mountain is well worth the effort for you will feel as though you can see forever.

At the lower regions there is lush vegetation where you may find scrumptious huckleberries to munch on. Also to be found are small headwater streams, some of which support fish life. These include the Middle and East Forks of Canyon Creek, as well as Strawberry, Berry, Onion, Redd, and Big Creeks.

Six of the seven lakes in the area also support fish life, the most popular being Strawberry Lake. Thirty-two acres in size, Strawberry Lake is the largest lake, furnishing the largest fish as a result. Because it is heavily-used the Oregon Department of Fish and Wildlife stocks the lake every four years with brook trout. Rainbow trout reproduce naturally. Other good fishing lakes (although the fish are small) include High Lake, the two Slide Lakes, and Little Strawberry Lake.

While fishing is certainly a popular pastime for those visiting the area, there are many other recreational opportunities available. In addition to backpacking, visitors can day hike, observe and photograph wildlife and scenery, explore, swim, horseback ride, and find that rare commodity—seclusion. During the fall, the area is used by deer and elk hunters. In the winter and spring months, folks visit the area on snowshoes and cross-country skis.

Another area of interest is the Canyon Creek Research Natural Area, located in the southwest portion of the Wilderness. A hike through should be a real treat for those who enjoy walking through large stands of ponderosa pine.

Archery enthusiasts may want to visit the Canyon Creek Archery Area. Established in 1940, a legal game animal consists of both buck and doe mule deer, as well as bull or cow elk, as long as they are taken with a bow. The remainder of the Wilderness is used for rifle and bowhunting for deer and elk.

There are about 150 miles of maintained trail linking various points, some of which follow the footsteps of the trappers, fur traders, and miners of long ago. Gold was discovered along Canyon Creek in 1862, and soon after miners arrived to establish their claims. Today hikers can still see many of these abandoned mines along the north side of the Strawberry Range.

Perhaps one of the greatest thrills to a hike in the wilderness is the chance to view wildlife. If you're quiet and lucky as well, you may see a variety of small and large mammals, as well as a quantity of bird life. Among the large animals are deer, elk, bear, cougar, and California bighorn sheep. (About 20 bighorn sheep live near the west end of Canyon Mountain.) Smaller mammals include porcupine, beaver, mink, and marten.

There are plenty of avian creatures to view also with over 100 species of bird life, many of which are migratory fowl, utilizing the area for nesting, feeding, or as a stopping-over site while heading north or south depending on the season. Look for blue and ruffed grouse, peregrine and prairie falcons, various species of owls, and golden and bald eagles to name a few.

A wilderness map, available for a small charge from the U.S. Forest Service, will help you in finding the above mentioned sites. Please note, however, that the current map shows the old wilderness boundary. There are plans to update the map and print a topographic map of Monument Rock Wilderness on the reverse side, but the Forest Service is not sure when this will take place.

For more information contact the following:

Malheur National Forest
Prairie City Ranger District
Prairie City, OR 97869
(503) 820-3311

or

Malheur National Forest
Forest Supervisor
139 N.E. Dayton Street
John Day, OR 97845
(503) 575-1731

Strawberry Mountain from the east

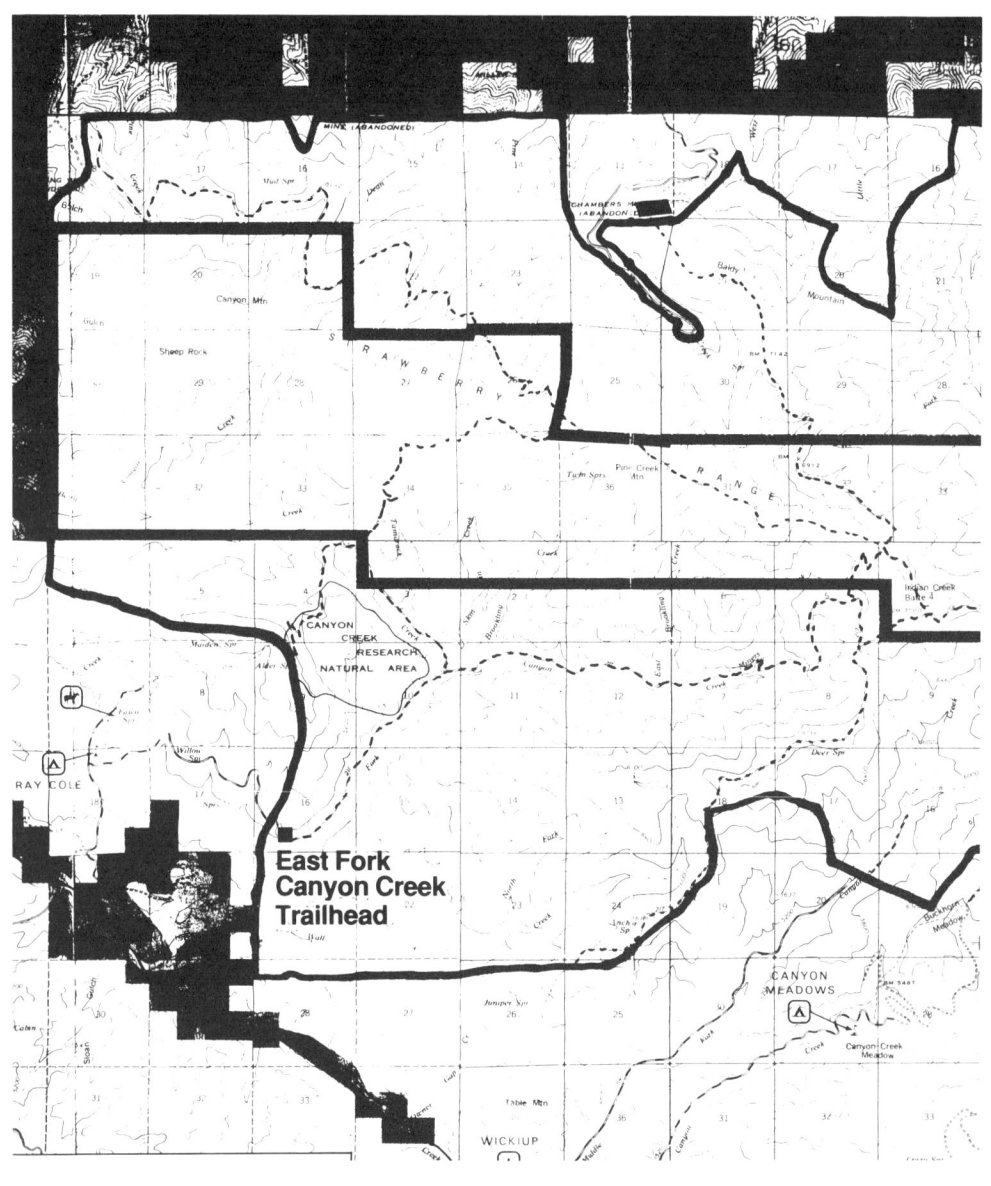

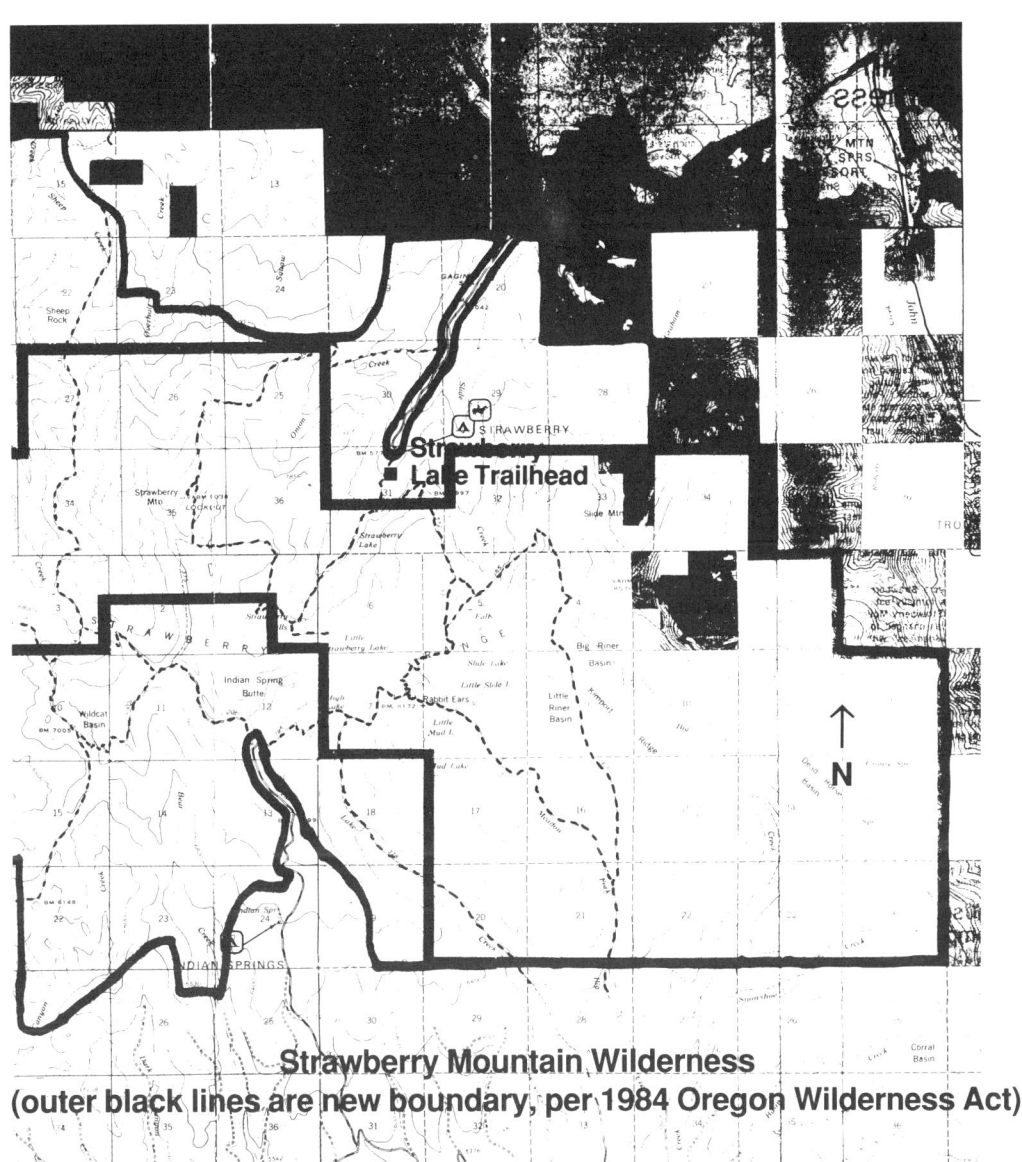

**Strawberry Mountain Wilderness
(outer black lines are new boundary, per 1984 Oregon Wilderness Act)**

33 STRAWBERRY CAMPGROUND TO STRAWBERRY MOUNTAIN

Distance: 6.2 miles (one-way)
Elevation gain: 3,265 feet; loss 0 feet
High point: 9,038 feet
Usually open: July through November
Topographic map: Strawberry Mountain Wilderness map
Obtain map from: Malheur National Forest

This hike is especially rewarding as the trail leads past Strawberry Lake, to the side and over the top of Strawberry Falls, through flower-covered meadows, and then there is a magnificent view from atop Strawberry Mountain.

To reach the Strawberry Lake Trailhead, drive U.S. Hwy. 26 to Prairie City, Oregon, located 13 miles east of John Day. Turn right (south) on Main Street, following the paved road and signs to Bridge Street (County Road No. 60) at 0.4 mile. Follow County Road No. 60 south for 6.6 miles (the road turns to gravel at the 3.0 miles mark) and reach a fork. Head left on FS Road No. 6001. Enter the Forest boundary another 1.5 miles down the road. Soon after this point pass McNaughton Spring Camp, a nice spot for camping, especially for those in need of horse facilities. Proceed 2.5 miles up the road to Strawberry Campground.

There are many shaded campsites at Strawberry Campground with plenty of room for tents or RV's. Picnic tables are provided for your convenience, as well as fire rings and pit toilets. As you enter the campground notice the parking area for visitors. Park here (unless you plan to spend the night at the campground) and reach the trailhead by walking down the road to the registration box. Please sign in and grab one of the trash bags provided for you if necessary.

Hike up the trail, entering the Wilderness in 200 yards. Strawberry Basin Trail No. 375 climbs through the trees at an easy, sometimes moderate grade to the junction of Slide Lake at 1.0 mile. Head to the right, passing another junction to Slide Lake just before Strawberry Lake. Keep to the right, reaching the north end of Strawberry Lake at 1.2 miles.

Spreading out across 31 acres, and reaching to a depth of 40 feet, Strawberry Lake, is an excellent spot for swimming or fishing. Anglers may catch brook or rainbow trout in the scenic lake. There are at least nine campsites located on all but the south end of the lake.

Continue through the trees around the east side of the lake, climbing moderately to Strawberry Falls at 2.5 miles. Switchback to the top of the falls, crossing over a bridge at 2.7 miles. Just ahead is the spur trail to Little Strawberry Lake, another good spot to catch brook trout. A 0.6 mile trail climbs an easy to moderate grade to the small lake. The fishing is good here, but the local fishermen suggest using a raft for best results. There are several campsites in the area. Look for one camp on the west end of the lake and another in the trees on the north end of the lake. Also, there is a camp located 100 yards up the meadow from the northeast end of the lake. In addition to these campsites you'll find another back at the junction. Shortly after passing the junction notice a rock cairn on the trail. There's a campsite just up the hill to the southeast about 100 feet.

To reach Strawberry Mountain continue straight ahead, following the trail to 3.0 miles. Walk to the edge of the ridge for a wonderful view of Strawberry Lake and other points below. Now the trail passes through high meadows with a wide variety of wildflowers including paintbrush, yarrow, crimson columbine and lupine painting the slopes.

Begin leveling off some as you reach another meadow at 4.2 miles. There are level campsites here and spring water nearby. This is an excellent spot for camping (good view also) for those that would like to continue to the top of Strawberry Mountain without a pack.

Continue on, skirting the edge of the meadow, and reaching an old cabin at 4.6 miles. There is another flat area here for camping and spring water nearby.

From here the trail begins a series of switchbacks across an open rock slope at a moderate to occasionally steep grade. Reach the top of the ridge at 5.1 miles. Hike the west side of the ridge reaching the junction of Onion Creek Trail No. 368 at 5.2 miles. Turn right onto Trail No. 368 and climb moderately then easy across the open shale slope that makes up the east side of Strawberry Mountain. Reach the junction to the top of the mountain at 5.9 miles. Turn left on Trail No. 368B, climbing moderately then up a few switchbacks to the top of the mountain at 6.2 miles.

On top of Strawberry Mountain discover tiny delicate wildflowers and maybe you'll see swifts darting about. Of course, there are spectacular views, too. See Ironside Mountain to the east, and Steens Mountain to the south. Those inclined to spend the night on the mountain will find the peak extremely rocky, but someone has cleared away the rocks on the east side of the peak, an area large enough for a sleeping bag or two.

Strawberry Lake

34 STRAWBERRY CAMPGROUND TO HIGH LAKE

Distance: 7.7 miles (one-way)
Elevation gain: 2,399 feet; loss 672 feet
High point: 8,172 feet
Usually open: July through November
Topographic Map: Strawberry Mountain Wilderness Map
Obtain map from: Malheur National Forest

Although there is a shorter trail to High Lake I'll describe this route because it allows for several side trips to a variety of lakes and the opportunity to hike through glacial-carved basins. Those who wish to visit High Lake via a one-mile trail can drive FS Road No. 1539 from the south and drop down to High Lake. If you decide to approach High Lake from the south you might be interested to know that at 8,060 feet, this is the second-highest road (passable by passenger car) in the state of Oregon.

To reach Strawberry Campground, drive U.S. Hwy. 26 to Prairie City, Oregon, located 13 miles east of John Day. Turn right (south) on Main Street, following the paved road and signs to Bridge Street (County Road No. 60) at 0.4 mile. Follow County Road No. 60 south for 6.6 miles to a fork in the gravel road (the pavement ended 3.4 miles from town). Head left on FS Road No. 6001 and enter the forest boundary another 1.5 miles up the road. Soon after entering the forest, pass McNaughton Spring Camp, a good camp, especially for those in need of horse facilities. Proceed 2.5 miles farther to Strawberry Campground and the trailhead.

There are plenty of excellent campsites here with Strawberry Creek flowing nearby. They are large enough for RV's and there are picnic tables, as well as fire rings and pit toilets for your convenience. There's a special parking area for visitors. Park here, unless you plan to spend the night at the campground, and proceed to the trailhead a short distance down the road. Please register at the trailhead and grab a free garbage bag if you'd like.

Enter the Wilderness about 200 yards from the registration box then climb the easy to moderate grade up Strawberry Basin Trail No. 375. The trail heads through the trees, reaching the junction to Slide Lake at 1.0 mile. Head to the right and reach another junction to Slide Lake just before reaching Strawberry Lake. If you'd like to visit Strawberry Lake keep to the right, reaching the north end of Strawberry Lake at 1.2 miles. Fishing and swimming are excellent here, but don't expect solitude as this is the most populated section of the Wilderness. Nine campsites are located all around the lake except at the south end.

At the Slide Lake/Strawberry Basin junction head left and hike the level trail to a fork at 1.4 miles. Head right on Slide Basin Trail No. 372 and climb moderately up the forest-covered slope. (At about the 2.0 mile mark look for Slide Mountain to the east.) Reach a junction at 2.4 miles. Just before the junction notice a trail to the left. Take the trail until it ends for a scenic lunch spot and a grand view of Prairie City, the Strawberry Basin, and more.

Back at the junction the trail to the right heads to Slide Lake, the one on the left leads to Big Riner Basin. Hike to the right on Trail No. 372 which is fairly level now. The trail crosses an open slope with an abundance of wildflowers in early summer and gorgeous views year-round. Notice the falls to the east before reaching a junction at 3.4 miles. Straight and to the left (down the hill) is Skyline Trail No. 385.

Enter the trees for a moderate hike to Slide Lake junction at 4.0 miles. Turn left and remain on the trail, staying to the right as you pass other trails heading off to the left. Reach Slide Lake, and the opportunity to hook brook trout at 0.2 mile. Hike to the south end of Slide Lake and over a small incline to Little Slide Lake. Little Slide Lake is only three acres in size, but is deeper than Slide Lake. Anglers will find brook trout in this lake as well.

There is an abundance of wildflowers around the lakes in the early summer months. Look for shooting stars and bull elephants head. There are a few campsites located between the two lakes with several other sites located around the scenic lakes.

Back on Skyline Trail No. 385 hike moderately up to a fork in the trail. The trail to the left switchbacks up to High Lake, but at a much steeper angle. Continue to the right, later climbing moderately up the switchbacks. Reach the junction of the Mud Lake Trail No. 379 at 5.7 miles. Head to the right, staying on Trail No. 385 and hiking short switchbacks up to a high point (8,172 feet) at 5.9 miles. There is a spur trail heading to the north for a fantastic 360-degree view. From this point see Graham Mountain, Slide Mountain, and beyond. Look down and to the west for a good view of High Lake nestled in a glacial cirque.

Begin a few long switchbacks down to High Lake at 7.7 miles. There are some good campsites around the south, west, and east ends of the five-acre lake. The lake is plenty deep for swimming (12 feet) and anglers will find small brook trout to hook.

High Lake

35 LITTLE RINER/MUD LAKE LOOP

Distance: 19.0 miles (complete loop)
Elevation gain: 3,944 feet; loss 3,944 feet
High point: 7,920 feet
Usually open: July through November
Topographic Map: Strawberry Mountain Wilderness Map
Obtain map from: Malheur National Forest

This trip allows for a peek at Strawberry Lake (or spend a day or more if you'd like) before heading up to Skyline Trail to catch some magnificent views from a splendid glacial-carved basin.

To reach Strawberry Campground drive Hwy. 26 to Prairie City, Oregon. Turn right (south) on Main St., following the paved road and signs to Bridge Street (County Road No. 60) at 0.4 mile. Follow County Road No. 60 south for 6.6 miles to a fork in the gravel road (the paved road turned to gravel 3.4 miles from town). Head left on FS Road No. 6001 and enter the forest boundary 1.5 miles farther. Soon after entering the forest pass McNaughton Spring Camp, a nice camp, especially for those in need of horse facilities. Continue 2.5 miles to the trailhead and Strawberry Campground.

Strawberry Campground is an excellent place to camp with plenty of room for tents and RV's, and the sound of Strawberry Creek flowing nearby. For your convenience there are picnic tables, fire rings and pit toilets. Park in the visitors parking area near the entrance (unless you plan to spend the night at the campground) and reach the trailhead by walking down the road to the registration box. Sign in and grab a trash bag if needed.

Begin hiking up Strawberry Basin Trail No. 375, entering the Wilderness in 200 yards. Climb the easy to moderate grade through the trees to the Slide Lake junction at 1.0 mile. Keep to the right and reach another junction to Slide Lake just before reaching Strawberry Lake. If you'd like to visit Strawberry Lake keep to the right, reaching the north end of Strawberry Lake at 1.2 miles. There are at least nine campsites located around all but the south end of the lake. Strawberry Lake gets a lot of use so don't expect solitude, but you can expect great fishing.

At the junction head to the left to reach Mud Lake and reach a fork at 1.4 miles. Take off to the right on Slide Basin Trail No. 372, climbing moderately up the forest-covered slope, looking for Slide Mountain to the east at the 2.0 miles point. Continue climbing to a junction at 2.4 miles. Just before the junction take the trail to the left for an excellent spot for lunch and a wonderful view of Prairie City, the Strawberry Basin, Slide Mountain, and more.

Back at the junction head to the right and toward Slide Lake. It's a fairly level hike across an open slope with lots of wildflowers in the early summer and wonderful views of the surrounding area. Notice the falls to the east before reaching a junction at 3.4 miles. Straight and to the left (down the hill) is the Skyline Trail No. 385.

Head back into the trees for a moderate hike to Slide Lake junction at 4.0 miles. Turn left and remain on the trail, keeping to the right when trails branch off to the left. Reach 13-acre Slide Lake at 0.2 mile. Hike to the south end of Slide Lake and over a small incline to Little Slide Lake. There are plenty of wildflowers near the two scenic lakes. Look for shooting stars and bull elephants head. Brook trout may be caught in both lakes and campsites are located between the two lakes and in a few other sites around the lakes as well.

Back on Skyline Trail No. 385 hike moderately up to a fork in the trail. The trail to the left switchbacks up to the Mud Lake Junction, but at a much steeper angle then the new trail. Continue to the right, later climbing moderately up the switchbacks. Reach the junction of Mud Lake Trail No. 379 at 5.7 miles. Head to the left, descending to the junction where the steep switchback ties in at 5.8 miles. Continue straight ahead for an easy hike to a creek at 7.1 miles. Cross the creek, reaching Mud Lake junction at 7.2 miles. Turn right to reach Mud Lake, 0.2 miles away. The lake is quite swampy around the edges with campsites being few and far between. There is a camp on the east side of the lake though.

Back on the trail, descend the easy to moderate grade through the trees passing a few meadow slopes as you go. Notice Meadow Creek flowing to the right of the trail. Cross a nearly dry creek at 9.5 miles, reaching the junction of Meadow Lake/Mud Lake 100 yards past the creek. There is a campsite near the junction and water from Meadow Creek which is nearby.

Head left up Meadow Fork Trail No. 376 climbing the moderate slope through the trees, sometimes crossing long, flat areas. Continue up to 11.2 miles where you will cross a small creek with a campsite located nearby. At 12.0 miles reach the top of a long climb. Walk up the ridge (off the trail) to the northwest for a view of Slide and Graham Mountains. There is a camp about 50 feet off on the opposite side of the trail.

It's a short, steep downhill then level to the Big Creek Trail No. 377 junction at 12.4 miles. From there head straight (Big Creek Trail to your right), climbing moderately to the junction of Meadow Fork and Skyline Trails at 12.8 miles. Head to the left on Skyline Trail No. 385, descending moderately then switchback across an open slope. Cross a stream at 13.8 miles then head back into the trees. The trail heads south at 14.2 miles and reaches a camp at 14.7 miles. There's an old corral here, a level site for a tent, and water at a nearby stream.

Continue an easy downhill to 15.7 miles and Slide Creek. Just before the creek notice the camp on the right. The falls cannot be seen from the camp, but can be seen from the trail before reaching the camp and from the meadow to the left as you cross the creek.

To reach the trailhead cross the creek, climbing to a junction at 15.9 miles. Turn right and continue up the easy grade across an open slope with lots of flowers and a great view. Reach a junction at 16.9 miles. Turn right on Slide Basin Trail No. 372, moderately descending to another junction at 17.9 miles. Turn right, reaching Strawberry Basin Trail No. 375 at 18.0 miles. Turn right again, and continue the easy to moderate descent back to Strawberry Campground at 19.0 miles.

EASTERN OREGON WILDERNESS AREAS

36 CANYON CREEK TO INDIAN CREEK BUTTE

Distance: 12.7 miles (one-way)
Elevation gain: 2,940 feet; loss 1,020 feet
High point: 7,500 feet
Usually open: July through November
Topographic map: Strawberry Mountain Wilderness
Obtain map from: Malheur National Forest

On this hike you'll travel through lush riparian growth along Canyon Creek, walk among giant ponderosa pines, stroll through an occasional meadow, and climb to the top of Indian Creek Butte for a terrific view of the surrounding area.

To reach the East Fork Canyon Creek Trailhead drive from John Day, Oregon. At the junction of U.S. Hwy. 395/U.S. Hwy. 26 in downtown John Day, head south on U.S. Hwy. 395 (S. Canyon Blvd.) for 9.8 miles. At this point turn left on FS Road No. 15 and travel 2.8 miles before turning left again on FS Road No. 1510. Drive 1.6 miles to FS Road No. 812, then proceed another 2.7 miles to the trailhead. There are hitching posts at the trailhead for interested horsemen or women.

Sign in at the trailhead then enter the Wilderness via East Canyon Creek Trail No. 211 a few yards thereafter. Gradually descend then level off before reaching Canyon Creek at 0.7 mile. It's an easy climb and descent to a camp at 1.0 mile. Gradually climb the easy ups and downs then level off again as you travel through a flower-filled meadow at 2.1 miles. Look for crimson columbine and other species amid the huge ponderosa pine found here. This stand of ponderosa pines is located in the Canyon Creek Research Natural Area.

Continue on, reaching a large camp area (Yokum's Corral Camp) at 2.3 miles. Farther on hike the level path to Tamarak Creek at 2.6 miles. A few hundred feet down the trail and you'll find Tamarak Camp and the junction of Joaquin Miller Trail. From here, it's a level or gradual climb to Brookling Creek at 3.0 miles and on to Bear Camp at 3.6 miles.

Press on, crossing another creek, then hiking up and down to East Brookling Creek at 4.8 miles. Climb the easy (sometimes moderate) grade through tall ferns shortly before coming to Miner's Creek at 6.0 miles. As you hike look for huckleberries along portions of the trail. Cross the creek several times before reaching a camp at the point where you cease to head northwest and instead head south. There's a flat spot for a tent and running water from Miner's Creek.

Continue up the switchbacks, then climb a moderate slope crossing four creeks before reaching a campsite at 7.6 miles. From this point there is a wonderful view of Indian Creek Butte, and if you're lucky you may see some birds and mammals in the meadow. There are several camps in this area with the most scenic one located just before heading back into the trees.

To reach Indian Creek Butte hike from the meadow, staying on Trail No. 211, and climbing moderately through the trees. Reach a camp, spring, and the junction of Table Mountain Trail No. 217 at 8.7 miles. Hike Table Mountain Trail across the stream then climb the moderate to steep grade to Table Mountain Cutoff Trail No. 217A at 9.2 miles. Just prior to the junction notice the gorgeous view.

Turn left on Trail No. 217A and climb the moderate to steep slope reaching an old boundary sign at 9.4 miles. Just after passing a large rock cairn (after a very steep uphill), hike off the trail and up the southwest slope of Indian Creek Butte for a magnificent view of the Butte itself, Strawberry Mountain range, and Baldy Mountain.

Back on the trail continue to 10.2 miles and the junction of Pine Creek Trail No. 201. Turn left on Trail No. 201 and gradually descend, watching for views of Strawberry Mountain and Prairie City to the north.

Reach another junction at 11.2 miles. Turn left on Table Mountain Trail No. 217, descending the easy to moderate slope with some good views of the Butte again. Reach the same camp and spring near Table Mountain Trail No. 217 at 12.7 miles. The loop around Indian Creek Butte is now complete.

Canyon Creek

INTRODUCTION TO THE WENAHA-TUCANNON WILDERNESS

Deep river canyons, broad tablelands, lava mesas and plateaus, and steep, sparsely vegetated valley walls, all combine to describe the rugged area known as the Wenaha-Tucannon Wilderness. If the area is visited sometime other than during the big game hunting season, solitude can also be found, as well as other sought-after wilderness values.

Located in northeast Oregon and southeast Washington, the Wilderness consists of 177,412 acres, 66,417 acres of which lie in Oregon. Because this guidebook deals only with Oregon wilderness areas we've excluded any hikes found on the 110,995 acre Washington side.

The Umatilla National Forest manages the area, originally created by the Endangered American Wilderness Act of 1978. In 1957, the Regional Forester designated a portion of the Wilderness-previously known as the Wenaha Back-Country and consisting of 99,000 acres—to provide an area in its undeveloped state for hunting, fishing, and camping. Later, in 1967, the Wenaha Back-Country area was enlarged to 111,244 acres and remained as such until inclusion in the Wenaha-Tucannon Wilderness.

Located in the Blue Mountains, the area ranges in elevation from a low of 2,000 feet along the Wenaha River to 6,401 feet atop Oregon Butte in Washington. Oregon's highest point appears to be an unnamed peak, rising 5,934 feet and located just south of the Oregon/Washington border on the west end of the Wilderness.

American Indians first inhabited this area. In fact, many of the areas 203 miles of trail originated from paths chosen by the natives. Later, around the late 1800's, the trails were used by cattlemen, sheepmen and trappers. Once the land was designated National Forest Land, trails were improved for fire control and grazing administration.

Today, elk hunters are the primary users of the trails. Those hunting or fishing in the Wilderness should remember that the area is located in two states. Hunting and fishing laws may vary according to the state.

A spring or summer visit is recommended. At this time of year, hikers and fishermen alike, are almost certainly guaranteed a true wilderness experience.

Summer temperatures (July through September) average about 80 degrees, but highs over 100 degrees are not uncommon. However, evenings are always cool, and pleasant for sleeping. Winter temperatures range from minus 20 degrees to 40 degrees above zero. Snowpack usually registers one to two feet along the Wenaha River, and eight to twelve feet at Oregon Butte.

A wide variety of trees dot the harsh terrain. Below 4,000 feet, hikers will mainly see a forest rich in Douglas fir, western larch, grand fir, Engelmann spruce, and Ponderosa pine. Above 4,000 feet, there exists primarily lodgepole pine and sub-alpine fir mixed with spruce, grand fir, and larch.

Wildlife in the Wenaha-Tucannon abounds due to the variety of habitat. With patience and luck, one might see part of the concentration of Rocky Mountain Elk in the area. Also, there are mule deer. Along the Wenaha River and its principle tributaries is one of Oregon's and Washington's more successful populations of whitetail deer.

Other year-round mammal inhabitants include the black bear, cougar, coyote, bobcat, marten, and numerous smaller species.

Birds abound in the Wilderness, with regular sightings of both the bald and golden eagle. Also, there are goshawks, coopers and sharpshined hawks, great horned owls, barred owls, and an assortment of woodpeckers, song birds, and ruffed and blue grouse.

Rattlesnakes are common in the area, especially near the lower elevations along the river and when hiking off the trail. Hikers should carry a snakebite kit.

For more information contact the following:

Umatilla National Forest
Supervisor's Office
2517 S.W. Hailey Avenue
Pendleton, OR 97801
(503) 276-3811

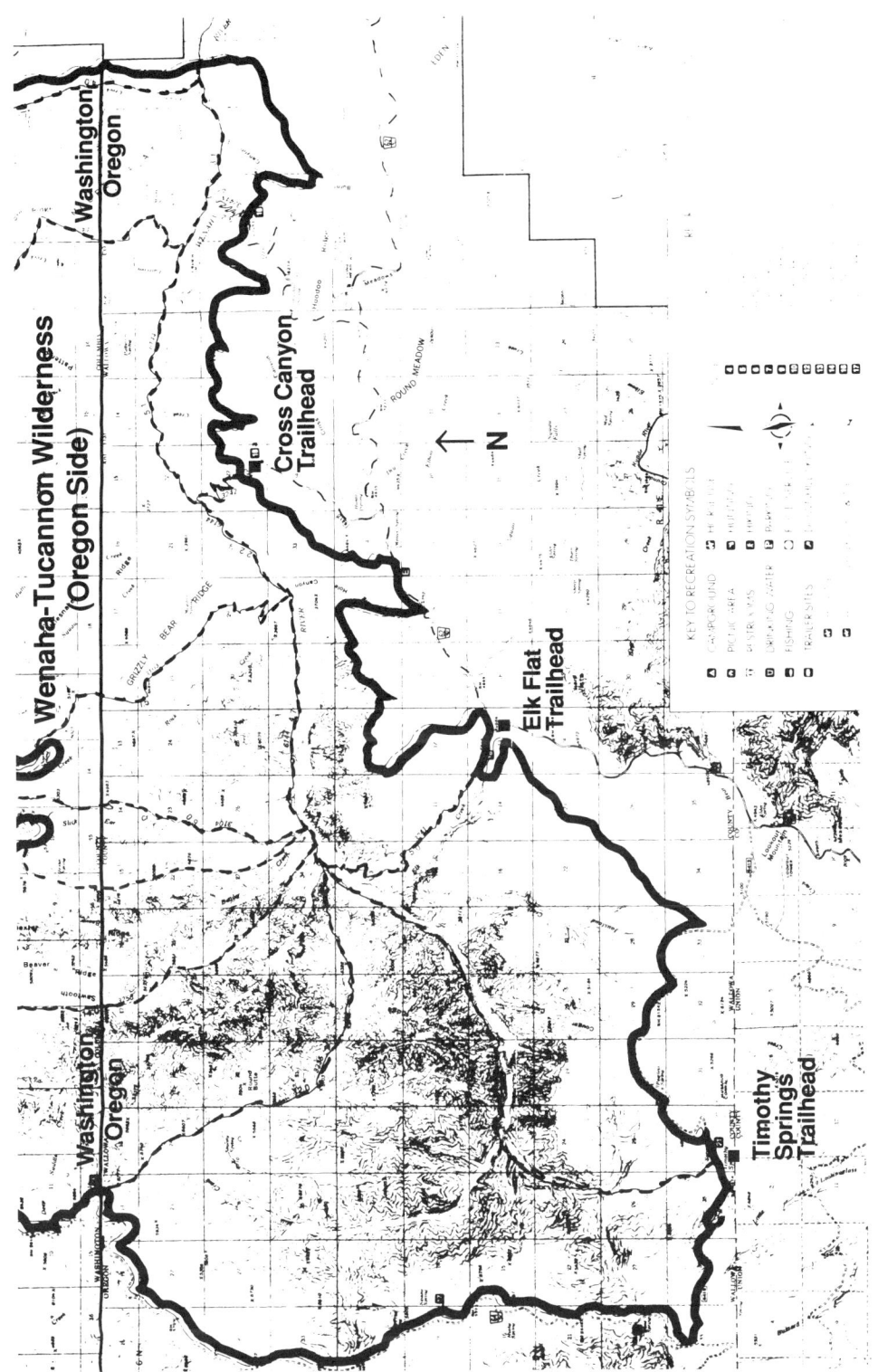

EASTERN OREGON WILDERNESS AREAS 107

37 CROSS CANYON TRAILHEAD TO WENAHA RIVER

Distance: 2.4 miles (one-way)
Elevation gain: 0 feet; loss 1,700 feet
High point: 4,100 feet
Usually open: June through November
Topographic map: Wenaha-Tucannon Wilderness Map
Obtain map from: Umatilla National Forest

In this guidebook there are three trails leading to the Wenaha River. Of the three, this hike is the steepest, but also provides the best in the way of views. Because much of the hike is across open slope, those hiking in hot weather may want to pick one of the other, more shaded routes.

To reach Cross Canyon Trail from Troy, Oregon (where you can buy supplies at a general store), go south toward Long Meadow. The road forks at 0.3 mile. Head to the right toward Long Meadow on FS Road No. 62 (Lookingglass-Troy Road). Drive 16.2 miles to FS Road No. 6217 and turn right. Continue 0.6 mile to the trailhead and end of road. Those hikers planning to day hike to the Wenaha River will find plenty of room to car camp at the trailhead.

The trail begins straight across from the stock loading area. As you head down the hill pass a wilderness sign about 100 yards from the trailhead. It's a moderate descent from here down to the river. Pass through forested slope and across open slopes where it's possible to get a good view into the river canyon. Also, there's a terrific view of Rattlesnake Ridge, across the river.

Reach the bottom of the canyon and a trail at 2.4 miles. Turn left and reach a campsite in about 100 yards. The camp is near the river. To hike the Wenaha River Trail ford the creek 100 feet west of the camp and catch the trail on the north side of the river.

Wenaha River

38 ELK FLAT TRAILHEAD TO THE WENAHA RIVER

Distance: 4.5 miles (one-way)
Elevation gain: 0 feet; loss 1,900 feet
High point: 4,900 feet
Usually open: June through November
Topographic map: Wenaha-Tucannon Wilderness Map
Obtain map from: Umatilla National Forest

Unlike the trail from Cross Canyon Trailhead (See #37, CROSS CANYON TRAILHEAD TO THE WENAHA RIVER), this hike is shaded for the most part, but does provide an occasional view as you descend to the river.

To reach the Elk Flat Trailhead drive from Troy, Oregon (supplies are available at a general store), and go south toward Long Meadow. The road forks at 0.3 mile. Head to the right toward Long Meadow on FS Road No. 62 (Lookingglass-Troy Road). Drive 20.2 miles to a dirt road and sign "Elk Flat." Turn right and reach the trailhead at 0.7 mile. There's an outhouse here and lots of room to camp.

The boundary for the Wilderness begins at the trailhead. The grade down to the river is moderate with one steep section and several easy sections as well. The trail heads primarily through old-growth forest—dense at times—with several semi-open sections where you can get a good view. Cross a dry creek at 3.5 miles.

While hiking down to the river look for ferns and moss which grow in the area, as well as wildflowers which bloom during the late spring/summer months. Reach the South Fork Wenaha River at 4.5 miles.

There is plenty of room for camping just before reaching the river. To reach the Wenaha River Trail, located on the north side of the river, cross the river near the washed-out bridge and continue on the other side until you reach the well-maintained trail.

Trail from Elk Flat to the Wenaha River

39 TIMOTHY SPRING TRAILHEAD TO WENAHA RIVER/ MILK CREEK

Distance: 4.1 miles (one-way)
Elevation gain: 200 feet; loss 1,500 feet
High point: 4,700 feet
Usually open: June through November
Topographic map: Wenaha-Tucannon Wilderness Map
Obtain map from: Umatilla National Forest

This hike is quite different from the other two Wenaha River hikes mentioned in this guidebook. Sections of the trail lead through lush vegetation, and portions pass through some relatively flat areas—quite a change from the moderate grades of the other two trails. Please note: Sections of this trail are moderate and steep, however.

There are two ways to reach the trailhead at Timothy Spring. From Troy, Oregon (supplies are available at a general store), go south toward Long Meadow. The road forks at 0.3 mile. Head to the right toward Long Meadow on gravel FS Road No. 62 (Lookingglass-Troy Road). Continue 25.1 miles to FS Road No. 6413 and make a right. Drive another 1.3 miles and turn right again, this time on FS Road No. 6415. (This is a dirt road not recommended for two-wheel drive in wet weather.) Take this to Timothy Spring Campground, another 6.4 miles down the road. Turn right to enter the campground, driving to the trailhead and end of road in about 0.2 mile. Timothy Spring is located off Road No. 6415, 0.3 mile east of the campground. There is a pit toilet, picnic tables, and fire rings at the campground.

To reach the trailhead from the south, head to Elgin, Oregon, where supplies are available. Drive north on Oregon Hwy. 204 for 20.1 miles, reaching FS Road No. 64 at this point. Turn right on the good gravel road and continue to FS Road No. 6411, 11.6 miles down the road. Turn left on Road No. 6411, a bumpy dirt road (passable by passenger cars), and take this to the junction of FS Road No. 6403 at 1.7 miles. Turn right, heading past Mottet Campground and piped water after 1.9 miles. Continue 1.7 miles to FS Road No. 6415. Make a right on Road No. 6415 and drive 4.4 miles to Timothy Spring Campground.

Enter the Wilderness at the trailhead and begin an easy hike down to a stream at 0.3 mile. At 0.5 mile cross another stream then hike up the short, steep grade and down again to another creek at 1.8 miles. Descend moderately to a point near the South Fork Wenaha River at 2.0 miles. Ford the river another 100 yards down the trail, then it's an easy up and down (though mostly down) to a couple more creeks at 2.5 and 2.9 miles.

Occasionally the trail leads across an open slope with the river far below. But most of the time the trail leads up and down, crossing another stream at 3.7 miles. At 4.0 miles begin a short series of switchbacks down the steep slope to 4.1 miles and South Fork Wenaha River/Milk Creek confluence.

Although there isn't much room to camp here, there is room on the opposite side of the confluence. Ford Milk Creek and find a nice campsite about 100 feet down and to the right.

Trail from Corral Creek to the Wenaha River

ACKNOWLEDGEMENTS

As with every project I undertake, I must first give thanks to God. For with God, all things are possible.

Next, I would like to thank my husband, Roger, to whom this book is dedicated. Although his heart isn't into backpacking like mine is, still he follows me up and down mountains, across countless streams and rivers, through dense vegetation, and over open slopes where the sun beats down relentlessly. Thank you Roger, for your companionship, support, and love. We've had some great times, haven't we?

And I must say thanks to our favorite backpacking pal, Samuel, our Samoyed. He adds so much joy to every journey.

Also, I have my family to thank. Nowhere in this world could there be a family that is more supportive, more loving, more caring, more wonderful. I thank God for them many times, each and everyday. To my Mom and Dad, Beverly and Don Ikenberry, and to my two brothers, Don and Dave Ikenberry, thank you for having faith in me, and for believing in me always. I'm so very proud of the closeness that we share.

A special thanks must also go to all of my friends, including my closest and best friends, Hoss and Lorraine Miller, Stan and Claire Thomas, Bruce and Doris Burney, Robert and Lyvonne Sewell. I'm grateful for your love, support, and encouragement.

In preparing this book I had to request a lot of information from various government agencies, particularly the U.S. Forest Service. Thanks to all those who replied with maps, answers to my many questions, and material on each wilderness.

Also, I mustn't forget Stephanie Hakanson, Aspenwood Studios. Thanks for a job well done in printing all of our black and white photographs.

And last, but never least, an extra-special thanks must go to Oral Bullard, my publisher, for his guidance and support, and for giving me the chance to do this series of guidebooks.

Donna, Sam and Roger